Designing the
Sustainable
School

Designing the Sustainable School

Alan Ford

images
Publishing

Published in Australia in 2007 by
The Images Publishing Group Pty Ltd
ABN 89 059 734 431
6 Bastow Place, Mulgrave, Victoria 3170, Australia
Tel: +61 3 9561 5544 Fax: +61 3 9561 4860
books@imagespublishing.com
www.imagespublishing.com

Copyright © The Images Publishing Group Pty Ltd 2007
The Images Publishing Group Reference Number: 727

National Library of Australia Cataloguing-in-Publication entry:

Ford, Alan B.
Designing the sustainable school.

Includes index.
ISBN 978 186470 237 8 (hbk.).

1. School buildings - Designs and plans. 2. Sustainable architecture.
I. Title.

727.047

Edited by Robyn Beaver

Designed by The Graphic Image Studio Pty Ltd, Mulgrave, Australia
www.tgis.com.au

Digital production by Splitting Image Colour Studio Pty Ltd, Australia
Printed in China by Whiz Group Limited, Hong Kong

IMAGES has included on its website a page for special notices in relation to this
and our other publications. Please visit www.imagespublishing.com

Contents

Foreword

Every morning, we send our children to school to learn, to explore, and to imagine—but we send them to buildings that are more like prisons than schools. In the U.S. alone, more than 55 million students and more than 5 million faculty, staff, and administrators spend hours every day in buildings with poor ventilation, inadequate lighting, inferior acoustics, and antiquated heating systems. For school superintendents or school board members, improving standards and raising test scores often takes priority over upgrading or maintaining facilities. But it's no longer an either/or question: high-performance green schools, like the ones featured in this book, are good for people, good for the bottom line, and good for the environment.

The benefits of building green schools are clear. First and foremost, children in green schools are healthier and more productive. As Mr. Eberhard notes in his essay, design features including attention to acoustical and visual quality, daylighting, and color have a profound impact on children's ability to learn. Green schools also have superior indoor air quality and thermal comfort, and expose our kids to fewer chemicals and environmental toxins, features that have been linked to lower asthma rates, fewer allergies, and reduced sick days. Green schools are also wonderful educational tools in and of themselves, serving as living laboratories to engage kids in the sciences, building arts, and environmental stewardship.

These benefits must be weighed against budgetary realities, of course—financing is often (mis)perceived as an obstacle to green design and construction. But as the 2006 study *Greening America's Schools: Costs and Benefits* shows, it costs less than 2 percent more to build a green school than to build a conventional, unhealthy, inefficient school—and that the financial benefits are 20 times as large. With dramatic reductions in energy and water use, and operations and maintenance costs, green schools can save $100,000 per year—enough to hire two new teachers, buy 150 new computers, or purchase 5000 new textbooks. The study, which was conducted by Capital E and sponsored by the American Federation of Teachers, the American Institute of Architects, the American Lung Association, the Federation of American Scientists, and the U.S. Green Building Council (USGBC), concludes that, "Greening school design provides an extraordinarily cost-effective way to enhance student learning, reduce health and operational costs and, ultimately, increase school quality and competitiveness."

Protecting the health of our children doesn't make much sense if we aren't also protecting the health of the planet they will inherit. Buildings have an enormous impact on our environment: in the United States alone, buildings use 12 percent of our water, produce 30 percent of greenhouse gas emissions, create 65 percent of our waste, and consume 70 percent of our electricity. But green buildings, like those that earn LEED™ certification from the U.S. Green Building Council on average use 30 percent less energy and 30-50 percent less water, reduce greenhouse gas emissions by 35 percent, and reduce waste costs by 50-90 percent. School buildings represent the largest construction sector in the U.S.–$80 billion in 2006-2008–which means that greening our schools affords us a tremendous opportunity to have a positive impact on our planet.

It isn't enough just to tell people about the benefits of green building and green schools. We also have to provide the building and education communities with the tools, knowledge, and resources to make green vision a reality. That's where USGBC and the Leadership in Energy and Environmental Design (LEED) Green Building Rating System™ come in. We are working to provide everyone who cares about our schools and school design–administrators, school board members, teachers, parents, contractors, architects, custodians, students–with the information and skills they need to build green schools.

USGBC was founded in 1993 to lead the transformation of the building industry to sustainable practices. Since USGBC launched the LEED Rating System in 2000, green building has exploded into the mainstream: the market for green building products and services is more than $7 billion, and USGBC's membership has increased ten-fold, to more than 7500 organizations. LEED has become the nationally accepted benchmark for the design, construction, and operations of high-performance green buildings. Nearly 6000 buildings, representing three-quarters of a billion square feet of building space, are registered or certified with LEED, and LEED is the tool of choice for organizations ranging from state and local governments to Fortune 500 companies.

LEED provides building owners and occupants with independent, third-party verification that a building meets the highest standards for health and performance. A voluntary system, LEED promotes a whole-building approach to sustainability by recognizing performance in five key areas of human and environmental health: sustainable site development, water savings, energy efficiency, materials selection, and indoor environmental quality.

Because school buildings have specific needs and concerns, USGBC has developed LEED for Schools, a green building rating system that recognizes the unique nature of school design and construction. Based on LEED for New Construction, LEED for Schools emphasizes issues including classroom acoustics, master planning, indoor air quality, and mold prevention in addition to issues such as energy efficiency and water conservation. The rating system is accompanied by a full suite of support resources, including a comprehensive LEED Reference Guide and schools-focused LEED workshops focused on school construction. LEED for Schools gives school administrators, school boards, community leaders, teachers, and parents the tools to have an immediate and measurable impact on the health of their children, the health of their education system, and the health of the environment.

Knowledge is power. And with books like this one, and LEED for Schools, we have the knowledge we need to transform the way we design, build, and operate our schools. It's time to put that knowledge into practice: if all new school construction and school renovations went green starting today, energy savings alone would total $20 billion over the next 10 years. We would create more than 2000 additional new jobs just from increased use of energy efficiency technologies. We would improve teacher retention and reduce dangerous air pollutants that cause respiratory disease.

Our children deserve to learn in healthy schools, and they deserve to inherit a healthy planet.

It's up to us to build them, so let's build green.

S. Richard Fedrizzi
President, CEO & Founding Chairman
U.S. Green Building Council

Neuroscience and the sustainable school

Research being undertaken by neuroscientists around the world is beginning to provide new insights into the influence that the qualities of schools have on learning experiences. Schools designed with an understanding of how the brains and minds of children respond to the attributes of spaces and places can lead to enhanced learning. Such research is adding to our architectural knowledge base an understanding of how daylight, acoustics, air quality, and views of nature are deeply influential on the cognitive processes of children.

Neuroscience–the study of the brain and the mind–is the fastest growing field of science today. Membership in the Society of Neuroscience has grown from 7000 a decade ago to more than 37,000 in 2006. Almost every university has a department or school of neuroscience; most are located in universities that also have architectural departments or schools. In the next decade there will be more and more efforts to bridge the current intellectual gap between neuroscience and architecture. The Academy of Neuroscience for Architecture (ANFA) was created in 2003 to assist both communities in building such bridges.

In February 2005, ANFA organized a workshop in San Diego for school architects, educators, and neuroscientists to explore concepts that might fall within the nexus of these three disciplines. Many of the building qualities addressed in this book were subjects for discussion by sub-groups of the workshop. The underlying premise of the workshop was that brain development between five years and twelve years of age is significant and progressively different each year. Cognitive psychologists and neuroscientists are intrigued with how cognitive capacities change with age. They know that regions of primary functions in the brain mature first, followed by complex/integrative task regions and eventually those regions that contain association areas for integrating information from several sensory modalities.

It was suggested that the workshop explore whether and how these changes in children's brains might require classrooms with differing attributes for each age. Several subjects explored in the workshop are also explored in this book. For example:

- ☼ **Good acoustics—noise and reverberation:** speaking and listening are the primary communications modes in most educational settings. Therefore noise levels and reverberation times of these learning spaces should be such that speech produced by teachers, students, and others is intelligible. Unfortunately, many learning spaces have excessive noise (unwanted sound inside or outside the room) and reverberation times.

- ☼ **Visual comfort—good stereoacuity and depth perception:** good visual function at close range, particularly good stereoacuity, is significantly correlated to academic performance. Results suggest that children with attention difficulties have a characteristic inability to restrict visual attention to a limited spatial area so as to selectively process relevant information while effectively ignoring distracting information.

- ☼ **Light—attention related difficulties, modulation of alertness:** studies show that lighting varies throughout the modern classroom. Inconsistency in the environment in schools can cause poorer performance on certain tasks. The brain processes light information to visually represent the environment but also to detect changes in ambient light level. The latter information induces non-image-forming responses and exerts powerful effects on physiology such as synchronization of the circadian clock and suppression of melatonin.

- ☼ **Color perception:** in addition to emotional associations, factors that affect color perception include the observer's age, mood, and mental health. Children who share distinct personal traits often share color perceptions and preferences. For example, very young children learning to distinguish colors usually show a preference for red or orange. It has even been suggested that specific colors can have a therapeutic effect on physical and mental disabilities.

Many of the schools featured in this book provide examples of the connections between sustainability and high-performance design. While these examples are not intended as an exhaustive checklist of possible sustainable features, they are buildings with rich design character whose qualities also provide environmentally responsible schools. In a future revised edition of the book I would hope that results of research in neuroscience would also provide scientific evidence for what today are intuitively understood design criteria.

John P. Eberhard, FAIA

Designing the sustainable school

There is probably no building type that has an impact on our lives in a more significant way than the K-12 school. We carry the memory of these places of early learning through the balance of our lives. As John Eberhard, FAIA notes in his essay for this book, the brain develops in very important ways during this time and the quality of school environments can play a crucial role in enhancing or impeding the learning experience.

Globally, school construction represents one of the largest sectors of new and renovation construction activity and therefore has significant environmental consequences. It also plays a major role in shaping the aesthetic experience and quality of life within our communities. Through the leadership of Rick Fedrizzi, CEO of the U.S. Green Building Council (USGBC), and the involvement of other concerned organizations, we have made great advances in being able to systematically address the issues of sustainability.

In addition to advancing our ability to design better schools, Mr. Eberhard and Mr. Fedrizzi share something else in common: both understand and address the issue of connectivity–mind to architecture and architecture to the environment. In Mr Eberhard's case, his work with the Academy of Neuroscience for Architecture (ANFA) has empirically demonstrated just how closely our minds and our environment are linked. Our immediate environment influences stress levels, alertness, physical and mental health, sense of self-esteem, and so on.

With regard to the connection of architecture to the environment, a core value of the Leadership in Energy and Environmental Design (LEED) system, which Mr. Fedrizzi helped to establish, is that we understand these linkages and find ways to learn from and work with the natural laws rather than against them when we design and build. There are great benefits to be gained by understanding these symbiotic connections. For instance, we are able to capitalize on the abundant available energy from the sun while understanding how the way light comes in a window has an impact on our mental state. The better we understand these inherent linkages, the more likely we are to find solutions that lead to enhanced learning and a sustainable future.

The vision

Designing the Sustainable School is a compendium of ideas illustrating how some very talented architects and committed facility planners are meeting the challenge of creating better schools for the 21st century. They are creating schools that are eco-friendly, embody high-performance design principles*, and are rich in architectural character. The projects selected for inclusion were chosen to represent a wide range of design solutions. It was my intention to represent aesthetic and geographic diversity among the projects as well as diversity of scale. Projects range in size from the Aga Khan Award-winning three-room schoolhouse in Gando, Boulgou, Burkina Faso by Diébédo Francis Kéré, to the 2500-student, 260,000-square-foot high school in Santa Ana, California by LPA Architects.

The work presented here utilizes a variety of sustainable guidelines including LEED, and Collaborative for High Performance Schools (CHPS) and, in the case of the Fossil Ridge High School, a sophisticated sustainable guideline developed by the local school district. Many of the projects are a result of architects and school facility planners taking the initiative to employ high-performance design principles independent of any specific sustainable structure or specification. Within the United States, LEED is quickly becoming the primary benchmark for designing and building green and a number of the projects featured here have LEED certification.

The tool kit

The high-performance "tool kit" utilized by the architects in this book is vast; a summary of sustainable features is included on the opening page of each project. Of these, the most frequently used tool is daylighting. In 1999 the Heschong Mahone Group produced a landmark study for the Pacific Gas and Electric Company (see the resource section for more information). The study involved more than 21,000 students and showed a dramatic correlation between daylit school environments and student performance. Proper use of daylighting may be the single most important tool in creating enhanced learning environments. When combined with high-performance glazing and automated electric lighting controls it also contributes to considerable energy savings.

Other high performance tools utilized include:

- ✿ **Water:** rainwater harvesting, on-site wastewater treatment, stormwater management, xeriscape landscaping, high-efficiency irrigation systems, biofiltration, water-saving plumbing fixtures
- ✿ **Energy:** photovoltaics, passive solar strategies, external sun shades, wind turbines, high-performance building envelopes, ground source geothermal combined with heat pumps, thermal mass, high-efficiency mechanical systems with web-based or computer controls, green roofs, "cool" roofs
- ✿ **Indoor air quality:** natural ventilation, solar chimneys, displacement ventilation, wind walls, use of low-VOC materials
- ✿ **Recycled and green materials:** construction site recycling, recycled content in building materials, certified green building materials
- ✿ **Transportation and multipurpose:** accommodation of alternative transportation systems, adaptable school plans that can evolve with changing educational strategies, and schools that serve as community centers for after hours.

This partial list gives some idea of the enormous strides being made in high-performance design, demonstrated by the projects presented in this book.

Imagine the possibilities

Architects often begin with the end in mind. We start by imaging the possibilities.

Imagine a school where the indoor air quality reduced the risk of exposure to disease, where the acoustics were such that learning was enhanced, where the quality of the finishes and architecture made you feel welcomed, valued, and nurtured, where the quality of light made you feel more alert and you did not have to turn on electric lights, where you felt connected to the outside world, where you generated the majority of your energy needs on site, where you promoted, taught, and practiced good environmental responsibility, where the school held a prominent and important place within the community, where test scores improved, where teacher retention increased and absenteeism dropped, where the school actually became a teaching tool …

The reality

Returning to a little dose of left-brain reality, all of this must be accomplished within limited budgets while solving the many complex spatial and regulatory needs that make up a typical K-12 learning environment. This is no easy task. As often happens, things have to be eliminated from the scope of improvements to comply with the available dollars for construction. The term often applied to this process is referred to as "value engineering." In the process of researching projects for this book I was informed by numerous architects that the first items to be "value engineered" out of their projects were many of the *imagined* items listed above. Fortunately, for the purposes of this book, there are plenty of examples where sustainability prevailed. Understandably, the first need in building schools is to provide shelter for the act of teaching/learning to take place. But, if we are to go beyond accommodation, then a major shift needs to take place in the area of values.

Furthermore, trying new ideas for achieving the high-performance school is fraught with risk. By its very nature, architecture, particularly school architecture tends to be conservative. Construction budgets are limited and the use of public funds dictates we are prudent with expending these funds. Risk aversion often overrides experimentation and new ideas are not attempted. If we are to accelerate our ability to produce the high-performance schools we all want, and need, we may need to throw a little more caution to the wind.

Conclusion

We will need leadership, community support and the political will to foster this change. With the tremendous broad interest today in "Green" and the efforts of organizations such as those listed in the resource section, we have the momentum to advance the possibilities of high-performance learning within eco-friendly environments. After all, this is ultimately about providing our kids with every tool we can imagine, and in the end, our future depends on it.

Alan Ford, AIA

* "High-performance design" and "sustainability" are often used interchangeably, depending on the source. For example, The Collaborative for High Performance Schools program embodies many of the same principles found in other sustainable guidelines such as LEED. As we typically use it in our architectural practice, high-performance design refers to the on-site design solutions that contribute directly to enhanced learning. Sustainability refers to strategies that use resources, both local and global, more efficiently.

Projects

Alexander Dawson Lower School

Boulder, Colorado, USA
Hutton Ford Architects

■ The lower school was the last new building completed in a ten-year campaign to completely revitalize the Alexander Dawson campus. The building accommodates 120 students in kindergarten through grade four. Although it is designed to function primarily as a stand-alone building, students do use other campus facilities such as the nearby gymnasium.

Every classroom has a combination of high translucent clerestories and low tinted-glass windows. These two opposite light sources provide well-balanced illumination throughout the day. The exact size and position of the apertures is optimized to avoid overheating while maximizing daylight. The high translucent clerestories are sloped inward to reduce contrast within the room and increase visual comfort. Electric lighting is very efficient but most teachers do not use it during the day. Other fully daylit spaces are the library, the music room, the kiva, and the cafeteria. Although the daylighting scheme is similar to that employed in the classrooms, each of these spaces has a slightly different section geometry to provide spatial interest and identity.

The project was a demonstration for a new green wood-based product called Parallam, made of waste wood fiber from the outer portion of logs. It is stronger and more reliable than typical wood products, including glue laminated timber. These structural components were used as exposed structure in the kindergarten, library, kiva, and music room.

Stone veneer used on the building matches other stone on campus and originates at a quarry near the project site. The stone is durable and has extremely low maintenance cost.

For watering the grounds, the school uses its own supply from agricultural ditches. Ditch water only flows for six months a year and must be used sparingly. Some irrigation water is impounded in two irrigation ponds on school property. Landscaping around the lower school is primarily Xeriscaping to conserve water and to provide educational lessons for students.

Sustainable features:

✿ Translucent angled clerestories in classrooms, with blackout shades ✿ Glass clerestories in kindergarten, library, and music room, with adjustable blinds ✿ High-performance tinted glass view windows ✿ Sloped ceiling to act as light reflector ✿ Exterior sunshades at library ✿ High-efficiency electric lighting: 0.86 watts per square foot maximum ✿ Dimming of fluorescent lighting in classrooms ✿ Local sandstone ✿ Parallam structural beams and trusses ✿ Porcelain tile flooring in high traffic and wet areas ✿ Xeriscaping except grass at playfield ✿ Highly efficient underground irrigation system ✿ Non-potable water used for exterior irrigation ✿ Low-flow plumbing fixtures ✿ Deep overhangs on south- and west-facing façades

1 North elevation

2 South and west elevations

3 View of south- and west-facing façades

4 Partial campus site plan

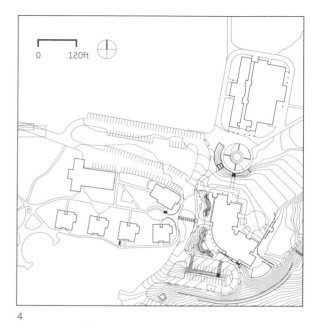

5

6

7

5   Loggia at library

6   Xeriscaping and campus entrance

7   Entrance from parking area

8   Commons are between gymnasium and lower school

9   View from playfields

9

8

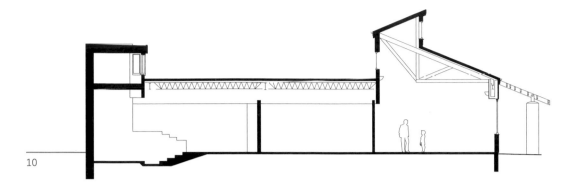

10

10   Section through library and reading kiva

11   Reading kiva

12   Typical classroom

13   Section at typical classroom

14   Kindergarten section

15   Kindergarten classroom with parallam trusses

Photography: Greg Hursley (3,6,9,10,12,13,15); Paul Hutton (7)

11

12

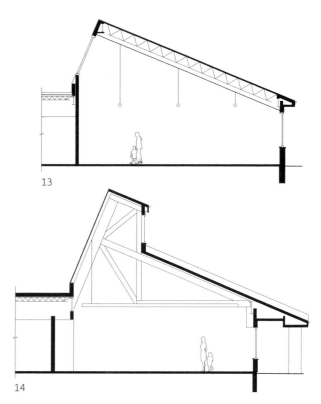

13

14

15

Alpharetta High School

Alpharetta, Georgia, USA
Perkins+Will

■ Stretching across a ridge in the foothills of the north Georgia Mountains, Alpharetta High School is a jewel of academic design excellence. In addressing a concern for the impersonal culture of large schools, Alpharetta High School is designed to support a "school within a school" concept. The school's population of 1850 students is divided between three classroom wings (or "houses"), where each wing is served by a core group of teachers. This smaller community, sharing the resources and benefits of a larger high school, allows faculty to personally know and guide the same group of students for their entire high school career. Students leave their houses for athletics, art, music, and career technology classes, and may switch houses for some language and science courses. However, the classroom wings were designed with the flexibility to support a variety of other organizational models as well.

The classroom wings open to a linear spine connecting the building's shared facilities: the media center, cafeteria, career tech components, arts, and athletic facilities. In response to the client's desire for a campus atmosphere, the arts and athletic facilities are located in separate buildings near the front door to facilitate public access during and after school hours.

Sustainable design is an essential part of Perkins+Will's design philosophy, thus every effort was made to be environmentally responsible at Alpharetta High School. Nearly all instructional areas receive natural daylight, building materials include recycled content and trees removed from the site were harvested through timber companies. In an effort to limit impact on the Big Creek basin and surrounding neighbors, site stormwater is controlled through a series of shallow rain gardens intended to help clean stormwater run-off from the building and parking lots and rehydrate the water table prior to leaving the site.

Sustainable features:

✷ Use of daylighting ✷ Use of recycled building materials ✷ Stormwater management strategies

1 Exterior

2 Exterior at dusk

2

1

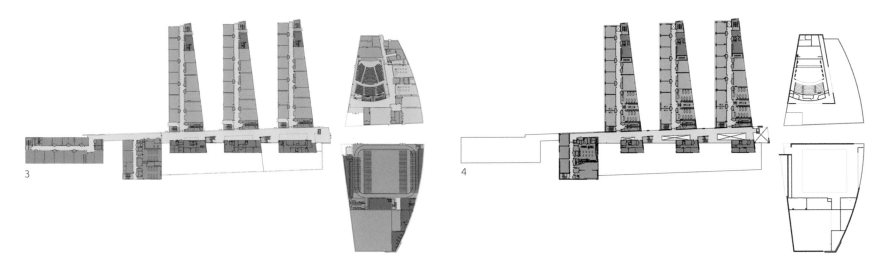

3

4

■ Career academy
■ Classrooms
■ Circulation
■ Administration
■ Athletics
■ Arts
■ Media center
■ Dining
■ Support

5

6

3 First floor plan

4 Second floor plan

5 Sustainable rain garden

6 Gymnasium

7 Cafeteria

8 Courtyard with students

9 Library

Photography: Christopher Barrett, Hedrich Blessing (1,2,8); Chris Little Photography (6,7,9); courtesy Perkins+Will (5)

7

8

9

American International School of Chennai

Chennai, India
Hillier Architecture

■ Hillier Architecture designed the 550-student American International School of Chennai (K-12) as a model of sustainable design. A fast-growing urban area about 10 degrees north of the equator, Chennai ranks as one of the world's largest and hottest cities. High temperatures, frequent power outages, and monsoon rainfall patterns pose significant environmental challenges. The design directly responds to these issues through careful orientation to the sun, judicious use of air conditioning, maintainable landscaping, and rainwater harvesting. To infuse the school with a local feel and provide students with a special sense of place, the architects used indigenous materials. The school is flexibly designed to accommodate future "green" solutions including fuel cell technology, solar panels, and reverse osmosis water treatment. With an area of about 220,100 square feet (20,450 square meters), the school is designed around a series of landscaped courtyards encircled by covered walkways. The courtyards and gardens open to the east to funnel cooling breezes throughout the building. Fountains provide evaporative cooling. North and south walls are deeply fenestrated, while east and west walls are nearly blank in response to virtually uncontrollable sun angles. Each classroom receives light and air from two sides, which is essential during frequent power outages. Rainwater is collected for irrigation and other suitable uses.

Each architectural element was carefully considered to take advantage of regional attributes and minimize cost and energy needs. Locally derived brick, granite, and sandstone, supported by poured-in-place concrete, form a maintenance-free exterior. Windows and doors are made from local teak; recycled bricks and terra cotta tiles mixed with concrete create an insulating roof slab that deflects and dissipates heat. A canopy of flowering vines grows on the armature of the building.

Sustainable features:

✿ Locally derived brick, granite, sandstone, and teak materials require little maintenance, and make the building of its time and place ✿ Oriented to mitigate harsh equatorial sunlight and provide natural cooling ✿ Classrooms receive light and air from two sides in case of power failures ✿ Deeply fenestrated north and south walls and covered walkways provide shade; blank east and west walls mitigate heat gain ✿ Courtyards and gardens open to east to funnel cooling breezes ✿ Fountains provide evaporative cooling ✿ Rainwater harvested to recharge aquifer and provide gray water for irrigation and toilets ✿ Flowering vines and other indigenous plant life create an "internal jungle" ✿ Flexible design to accommodate future fuel cell technology, solar panels, and reverse osmosis water treatment

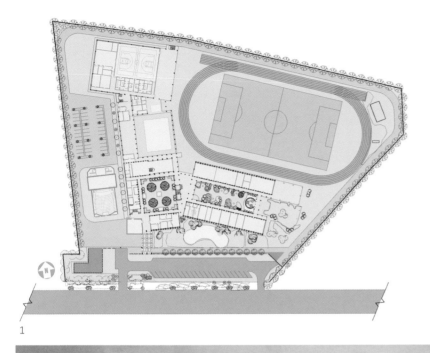

1 Site plan

2 Exterior of the school from the street

3 Detail of wall: deeply fenestrated north and south walls protect against heat gain

4

5

6

4   Retention pools collect water for irrigation and other suitable uses

5   View of pool

6   Interior courtyard designed to maximize shade and funnel cooling breezes

7   Open-air corridors provide shade and funnel cool afternoon breezes

8   Courtyard with flags: indigenous plants and a fountain provide cooling

Photography: Nicholas Garrison, AIA, LEED ap

7

8

The Anglo-American School – Sofia

Sofia, Bulgaria
Hillier Architecture

Located on a rolling plateau at the base of suburban Sofia's Mount Vitosha, the new 500-student Anglo-American School - Sofia (K-12) was designed to be a "best practice" environmental school. Ecological and specific "green" considerations are part of the school's core philosophy and the design showcases these themes. Built of natural local materials and inspired by regional design traditions, the school manages its use of water, daylight, energy, and local vegetation to create a total learning environment.

Conceived of as a village, each "wing" of the 280,000-square-foot (26,000-square-meter) school is distinguished by a different color, a polychromatic design motif visible in the local architecture. The school compound is set low into the site in order to reduce wind resistance and improve the spectacular "up hill" southern views toward majestic Mount Vitosha. Flat roofs are covered in local sedum to create evergreen roofscapes that merge with the beauty of the hillsides.

Daylight is carefully controlled to filter into all classrooms. Roof monitors double the average daylight into the rooms, rendering artificial light mostly unnecessary. On the south faces of the classrooms, passive solar shading is achieved in the form of climbing roses, an indigenous flower and one of Bulgaria's most important cash crops. Demonstration solar panels, water collection cisterns, and bird feeding gardens, combined with active weather monitoring stations and observatories for star gazing, allow students to be partners with their natural environment. This approach turns the school into a "living laboratory" that teaches students to appreciate and respect the world they inhabit.

Sustainable features:

✿ Sited to reduce wind resistance, maximize daylighting, and take advantage of mountain views ✿ Village layout and polychromatic design influenced by regional architecture ✿ Evergreen roofscapes blend with the hillside ✿ Local materials minimize cost and environmental impact ✿ Roof monitors double average daylight in rooms ✿ Cisterns recycle rainwater ✿ Indigenous climbing roses provide passive solar shading ✿ Bird-feeding gardens, weather monitoring stations, and demonstration solar panels engage students in learning about their environment

1 East elevation

2 Courtyard view

East Elevation

1

2

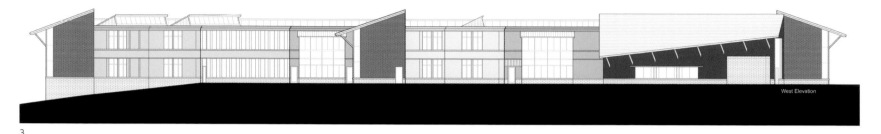

3

4

Photography: Andy Lang

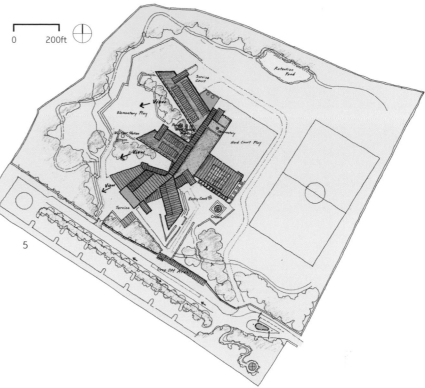

5

6

7

Ash Creek Intermediate School

Monmouth, Oregon, USA
BOORA Architects

Flexibility, connectivity, and sustainability are the hallmarks of the 58,919-square-foot (5474-square-meter) Ash Creek Intermediate School. Initially accommodating only fifth and sixth graders, Ash Creek has been designed to eventually house kindergarten through fifth grade as the Central School District completes the final stages of its current long-range facility plan. To minimize disruptions to classrooms, the media center, and the multipurpose rooms when this change occurs, sinks and counters were mounted on tracks that easily adjust to different heights and cabinets were installed that can be easily moved to new positions. In addition, interior spaces are flexible: the cafeteria doubles as an auditorium/theater, and recesses of the hallways become informal meeting areas.

Interior spaces have also been designed to foster a sense of interconnection between indoor and outdoor areas. Internal classrooms share daylight that streams in through perimeter spaces via interior clerestories and wide expanses of glass. These same windows also allow constant views to the wetlands preserve and playfields surrounding the school, supporting the school's close relationship to the environment. Further, Ash Creek maintains active ties with the community, offering playfields, PE spaces, meeting rooms, and academic areas for community use.

Sustainable and high-performance design elements, such as exterior light shelves that bounce light deep into the facility, natural ventilation, low off-gassing finishes, durable materials, and energy efficient systems, would garner the school a LEED Silver rating if certification was pursued. More importantly, however, these sustainable design strategies reduce the facility's energy costs by more than 35 percent.

Sustainable features:

☼ Wetlands preserve on site ☼ Exterior light shelves bounce light deep into the facility ☼ Natural ventilation ☼ Low-VOC finishes ☼ Durable materials ☼ Energy-efficient systems ☼ Designed to LEED Silver certification ☼ Energy costs reduced by 35% ☼ Skylights, clerestories, and interior glazing allow interior spaces to share light ☼ Classrooms are partially illuminated by Solatubes, mirrored directable units that channel light from the exterior to interior spaces and distribute it internally via small lamp-like apertures in the ceiling ☼ Entry canopy shades expansive glass on the east side of the building

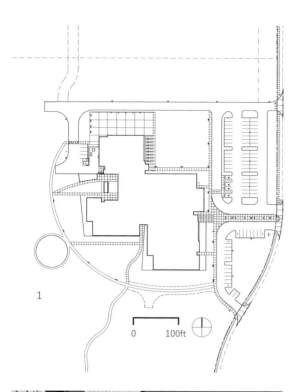

1 Site plan

2 Clear glass above the light shelves and tinted glass below maximize the available light reflected into classrooms in cooler months while reducing excess heat and glare during the summer

3 Entry canopy shades expansive glass on the east side of the building

4 Clerestories, windows, and glazed doors, as shown on the exterior of the gymnasium, are used extensively as a daylighting strategy

0   100ft

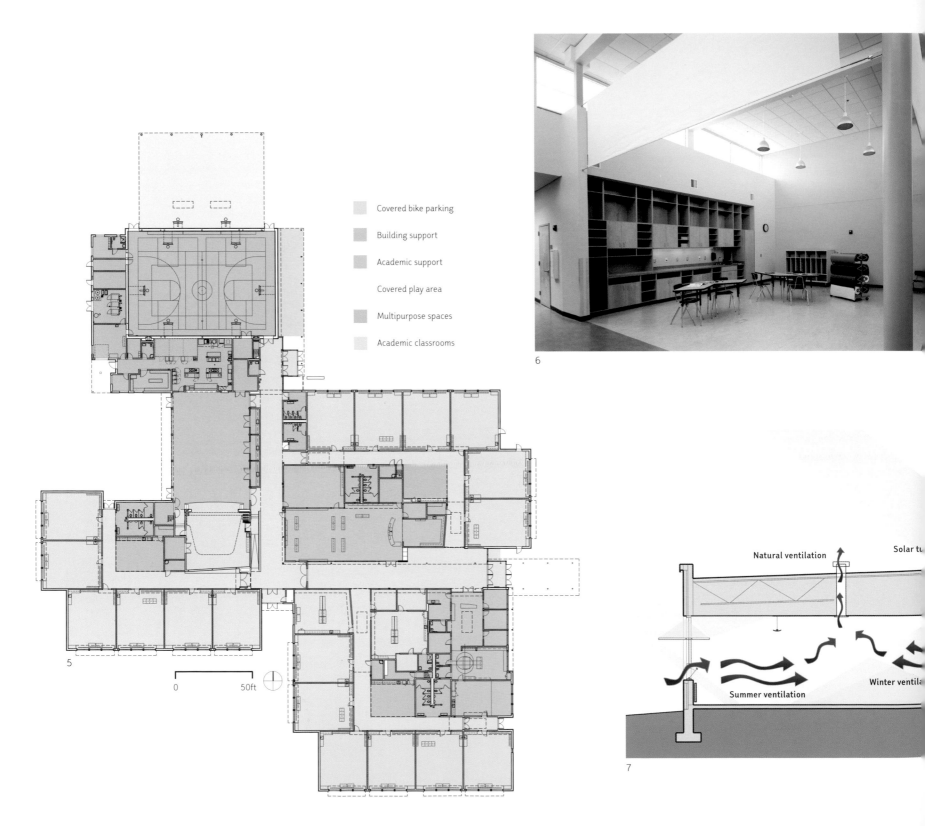

Covered bike parking

Building support

Academic support

Covered play area

Multipurpose spaces

Academic classrooms

0   50ft

5

6

Natural ventilation   Solar tu

Summer ventilation   Winter ventila

7

5 Floor plan

6 Clerestory windows in a
   multipurpose space

7 Building section at classroom
   showing natural ventilation
   sequence and daylighting path
   through windows, light shelves, and
   interior and exterior clerestories

8 Clerestories, windows, and glazed
   doors at the entrance to the
   gymnasium

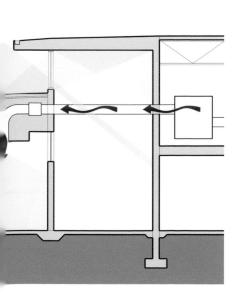

9

11

10

9 Classrooms are partially illuminated by Solatubes, mirrored directable units that channel light from the exterior to interior spaces and distribute it internally via small lamp-like apertures in the ceiling

10,11 Skylights draw light into the media center

12 Skylights draw light into the media center

12

Photography: Sally Painter for BOORA Architects

Aspen Middle School

Aspen, Colorado, USA
Studio B Architects
Hutton Ford Architects

■ The Aspen School District emphasizes creative classroom learning, outdoor education, safety, and sustainability and therefore wanted this new middle school building to echo its commitment to students and environmental responsibility. Additionally, the ASD wanted a building that would unify the tri-school campus and replace an aging, leaking, outdated, and inefficient middle school. The new middle school supports the Aspen School District's progressive educational mission and curriculum with a modern 110,000-square-foot (10,220-square-meter) LEED certified building.

The new L-shaped building wraps around the existing middle school not only to maintain existing school operations during construction of the new building, but also to replace the current building with a new larger, safer, sun-filled playground environment. The new environment includes ample daylighting, improved ventilation, new building and technology systems, better access and security, and views and spaces that connect the building's users to the surrounding mountain landscape.

The architectural language reflects the direction of an educational program focused on a sustainable future. Wherever possible, LEED certified green materials such as bamboo and recycled content flooring are incorporated into the design. Aluminum-framed, high-performance glazing provides natural light to all educational spaces. Window openings and sunshade devices respond to solar orientation, and create a distinctive aesthetic. An extended canopy identifies the main east-facing entry, and the adjacent arcade provides a safe, visible, protected shelter for student drop-off and pick-up. Selected high-efficiency mechanical, electrical, and plumbing systems that integrate innovative products and techniques such as solar air heating, waterless urinals, and solar tubes will make this the most energy-efficient classroom building on the school campus. These strategies will result in reducing carbon dioxide by almost 1 million pounds per year.

Sustainable features:

☼ Green, recycled, and low-maintenance materials used where possible ☼ High-performance glazing ☼ Window openings and associated shading devices respond to solar orientation ☼ High-efficiency mechanical and electrical systems ☼ Solar air heating ☼ Waterless urinals ☼ Solar light tubes ☼ Photovoltaic panels ☼ Natural daylighting in all classrooms ☼ Access to views and outdoor spaces ☼ Automated electric lighting controls

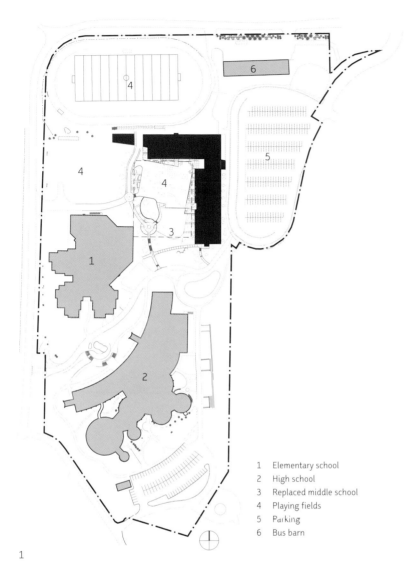

1   Elementary school
2   High school
3   Replaced middle school
4   Playing fields
5   Parking
6   Bus barn

1   Campus site plan

2   Southwest elevation and playground

3   Southwest entry and cafeteria terrace

4   Northeast main entry and library

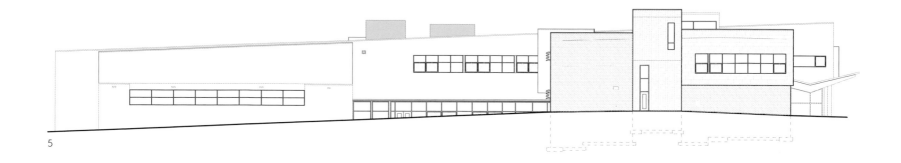

5

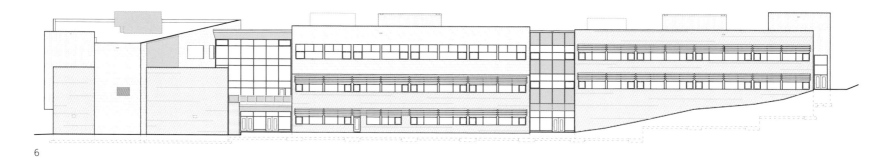

6

7

5   South elevation

6   West elevation

7   East elevation and classroom wing

8   Northeast view of administration and library

9   View from cafeteria terrace toward classroom wing

10   View from lobby toward cafeteria terrace

8

9

10

11 Main lobby

12 View from main lobby into classroom wing

13 Main lobby

14 Typical classroom

Renderings: courtesy Studio B Architects

12

11

13

14

Benjamin Franklin Elementary School

Kirkland, Washington, USA
Mahlum Architects

Sustainable features:

✧ Building envelope and HVAC performance 35% better than state energy code ✧ All learning areas are naturally ventilated; operable windows and ventilation chimneys utilize a natural stack effect ✧ Operable windows and automatic controls for optimum indoor air quality. CO2 and occupancy sensors adjust louvers located below the windows and at the upper levels of the ventilation stacks to provide ventilation and conserve energy ✧ East-west orientation with major glazing on the north and south elevations to maximize natural daylight; automatic dimming adjusts light levels in the classrooms to maximize energy efficiency of natural light ✧ Durable, non-toxic, low-impact finish materials including low-VOC paint, rubber resilient flooring, wool tackable wall coverings, retroplated concrete floors, ground face concrete block, cement board siding, and recycled glass cullet ✧ Low-flow and low-flush plumbing fixtures; waterless urinals save an estimated 60,000 gallons (227 cubic meters) of potable water per year ✧ Central courtyards expose students to art, elements of the region's unique hydrologic process, and provide direct connections to the site's native forested ecosystem; site-specific, native, and drought-tolerant plantings require no permanent irrigation ✧ Low-impact development (L.I.D.), "rain-garden," strategies collect stormwater on-site through point-source bio-retention systems; planted collection cells for on-site stormwater management maximize infiltration and ground water recharge, water quality filtration, and evapotranspiration while minimizing discharge rates

■ Learning is about creating connections. That's one reason why the new 56,000-square-foot (5202-square-meter) Benjamin Franklin Elementary School was designed to connect students directly with the environment in which they live.

The new public school replaces an existing facility on a narrow 10-acre (4-hectare) site that is oriented north–south. The surrounding residential neighborhood is interlaced with equestrian trails, horse paddocks, and forested lands, including a mature stand of Douglas fir that covers the northern third of the property. This rich natural setting and a requirement to maintain operation of the existing school during construction led to the new facility's location at the center of the site, embracing the woods.

The natural environment extends into the school's two central courtyards. These structured outdoor learning environments expose students to art, elements of the region's unique hydrologic process, and direct connections to the site's native landscape. The functional ecosystem of the southern courtyard makes natural processes visible on a day-to-day basis. Highlighting subtle environmental variations in sun, wind, rain, and shadows, this setting provides a lens through which visitors of all ages can view the intricate workings of the environment in which they live.

Inside, the school's 450 students in grades K–6 are distributed within small learning communities formed by clusters of four naturally ventilated and daylit classrooms around a multipurpose activity area. Stacked within two-story wings that extend toward the woods, these communities are integrally linked with views and access to nature beyond.

A proactive initiative by the Lake Washington School District that anticipated forthcoming legislation to mandate sustainable practices at the state's publicly funded schools, this high-performance facility provides the district with an exemplary model for future development. Benjamin Franklin Elementary School expands learning beyond the classroom by connecting the district's educational pedagogy with environmental sustainability at every level.

1

2

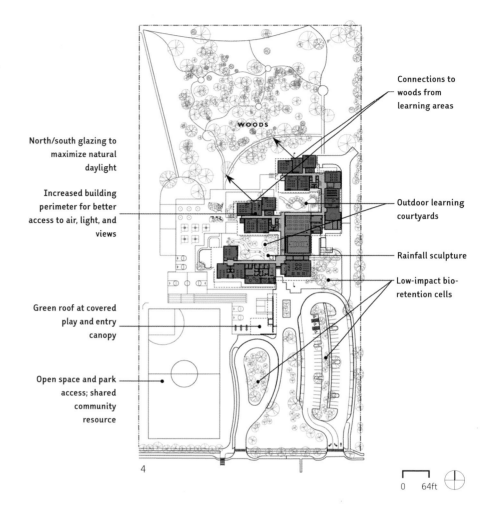

North/south glazing to maximize natural daylight

Increased building perimeter for better access to air, light, and views

Green roof at covered play and entry canopy

Open space and park access; shared community resource

WOODS

Connections to woods from learning areas

Outdoor learning courtyards

Rainfall sculpture

Low-impact bio-retention cells

4

0   64ft

3

1   Naturally daylit gym and commons with connection to the north courtyard beyond

2   South courtyard with native plantings and adjacent classroom cluster

3   Classroom cluster from outdoor play area

4   Site plan

5   First floor plan

6   Library with clerestory windows that provide balanced daylighting and relief air for the natural ventilation system

7   Moveable and glazed doors connect the classrooms to the activity area

8   Activity area with connections to surrounding classrooms and wooded area

9   Typical classroom cluster building section

Photography: Benjamin Benschneider

Perimeter hydronic heating and ventilation louvers

Operable windows

Natural ventilation chimneys

North/south glazing to maximize natural daylighting

Overhead clerestory for daylighting and ventilation

Interior lightshelves and exterior sunshades for solar control

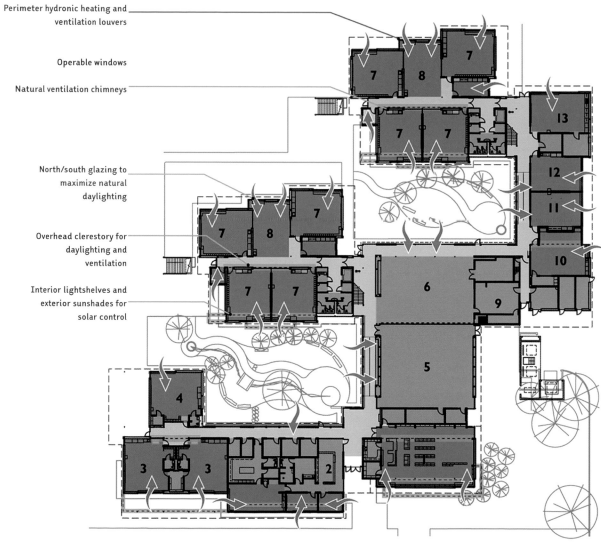

6

1   Library
2   Administration
3   Kindergarten
4   Early childhood
5   Gymnasium
6   Commons
7   Classroom
8   Activity area
9   Food service
10 Music
11 Resource
12 Technology
13 Science/art

0   32ft

5

7

8

AUTOMATIC DIMMING
LIGHTING-CONTROLS

CLERESTORY
WINDOWS
& LOUVERS

INTERIOR
LIGHTSHELVES &
EXTERIOR
SUNSHADES FOR
SOLAR CONTROL

PERIMETER HYDRONIC
HEATING & VENTILATION
LOUVERS

NATURAL
VENTILATION
CHIMNEY

OPERABLE WINDOWS

INDIRECT
SUNLIGHT

DIRECT
SUNLIGHT

DIRECT
SUNLIGHT

VIEWS

FOREST

ACTIVITY AREAS

CLASSROOM

COURTYARD

VIEWS

VIEWS

ACTIVITY AREAS

CLASSROOM

VIEWS

9

Berkeley Montessori School

Berkeley, California, USA
Pfau Architecture, Ltd.

■ This design attempts to balance the opportunities presented by its urban context, the surrounding building site, the historic Santa Fe train station, the needs of a Montessori teaching environment, and a strong concern for the creation of a sustainable building. It also balances a thoughtful and flexible plan for addressing budgetary constraints with the need to create a stimulating, flexible, and playful environment for the children.

Every effort is made to connect this new Montessori community to the Berkeley community at large and the fabric of the surrounding neighborhood. The courtyard created by the building massing is open to the south, providing light and a visual connection to the adjacent park. Drop-off is at the northeast corner of the site, allowing a shared turn-out off University Avenue with the synagogue next door, as well as shared queuing. The western edge of the site is given over to the bicycle and pedestrian path that connects with the "safe routes to school" city-wide linkage of paths and green spaces. Parking is provided, in a concentrated manner, at the front of the site where it shares access with the drop-off and minimizes the amount of site usage.

The creation of useful outdoor space with a constructive relationship to interior space was a prime objective of the scheme. The new architecture was linked to the old by creating a new take on the central courtyard gathering space, with plantings that reflect the mix of cultures and history that form California's heritage. A series of experiential processes are used to activate the senses. All are derived from natural forces, the elements that act upon the earth in order to create a greater awareness of our place in history and time and space through experiment.

Sustainable features:

✿ Rooftop solar water heating and in-floor radiant heating, which is ideal for children "doing work" on the floor ✿ Hot water from the roof is stored in a holding tank prior to circulation through the system, providing heat storage capability to fill in the gaps in solar gain ✿ Orientation of building assists daylighting, ventilation, and solar heat generation ✿ Cooling is provided by two types of natural ventilation: operable windows oriented to prevailing winds on the lower level, and stack effect through multiple light monitors on the upper level ✿ Natural daylighting is enhanced by creating a shorter distance between the windows on either side of the classroom and north light monitors located on the roof; if possible, these systems could be assisted by on-site power generation by photovoltaic panels and wind generation resulting in reverse metering ✿ Sustainable building materials used where possible, using low fly-ash concrete, certified woods, and recycled material building products ✿ The building is targeted to achieve the highest possible level of LEED certification ✿ Plant selection and planting design attempt to accommodate students', teachers', and parents' many needs and at the same time make the school garden a successful learning tool, as well as a safe, sustainable, and attractive environment ✿ The master plan incorporates a gray water irrigation system

1

2

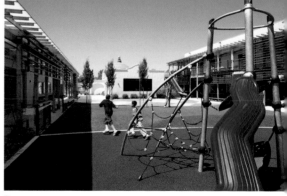

3

1   View of the school and the historical
    Santa Fe train depot from University
    Avenue

2   Looking down onto the center courtyard,
    lower elementary school building, and
    the historic train station from the middle
    school level

3   Looking across the courtyard toward the
    upper elementary and middle school
    building from the lower elementary
    building

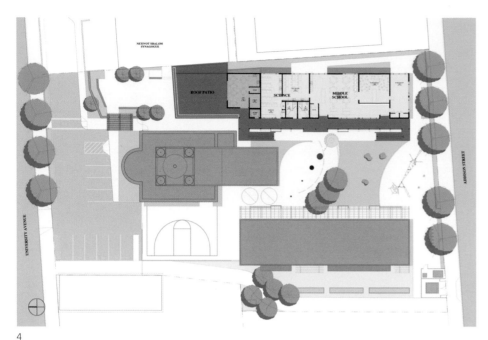

4

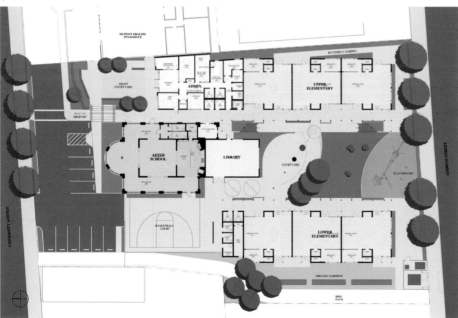

5

4 Upper floor plan

5 Ground floor plan

6 View of the back of the school as seen from a nearby neighborhood park

7 Stair leading up to the middle school level from the lower level

8 Middle school second floor exterior walkway

9 View from lower elementary corridor looking toward the middle school building—all buildings feature wood louvers for sun shade

6

8

7

9

10

10 Children playing in courtyard with the lower elementary school building in the background

11 Courtyard at the front of the school where children wait for their parents

12 Middle school science classroom

13 Lower elementary classroom with abundant access to natural light

Photography: Paul Dyer

11

13

12

The Business Academy, Bexley

London, UK
Foster + Partners

The Business Academy, Bexley is an innovative building that stretches the boundaries of education. It is part of the British government's radical new approach to raise educational standards in areas where there are problems of under-performance and is the first purpose-built, part-privately funded independent state school in Europe.

The architectural approach comes from the philosophy of schools regeneration company, 3Es. This philosophy demands open, transparent, and compact spaces to encourage integration, communication, and cross fertilization between students of all age groups, students and teachers, students and visitors, and all the different educational disciplines in the curriculum. It forges intimate links with the local community to provide a safe, exciting, and enjoyable environment for out-of-hours, extra-curricular activities.

Working within the framework of the Department for Education and Skills guidelines, Foster + Partners developed an open-plan compact design based around three courtyard spaces devoted to business, art, and technology.

The courtyard spaces visually and functionally link teaching spaces on different levels as well as teaching spaces of different educational disciplines. The teaching spaces are separated from each other only by partitions (which are intended to be moved to change the sizes of teaching areas or adapt them for other uses) but open to circulation space and courtyard space. There are no corridors and circulation occurs through the business court, art court, and technology court at ground level or along the courtyards at levels one and two.

The building is capable of reducing heat loss in the winter and, through its unique double-layered facade with external shading louvers that automatically track the sun's path, capable also of reducing heat gain during the summer to provide optimum conditions and minimize the building's energy use.

Sustainable features:

⚙ Auto-tracking sun shades to optimize daylighting and energy performance ⚙ Manual override on sun shade tracking system at each classroom permits individual control for differing educational needs ⚙ Double-layered façade for improved energy performance ⚙ Compact design to reduce energy loss ⚙ Flexible plan to allow adaptability for changing educational needs ⚙ Natural ventilation at teacher support areas to reduce cooling load

1

2

1,4 Entrance

2 Site plan

3 Exterior view

4

3

5

5,7 Atrium

6 Art courtyard

6

7

8

8   Interior view of floor level

9,10   Interior view of art courtyard

Photography: Nigel Young/Foster + Partners

9

10

Capital City Academy, Brent

London, UK
Foster + Partners

Academies are a new kind of secondary school initiated by the British government and supported by entrepreneurial sponsors who contribute 20 percent of the initial capital costs. The academies offer a free education of the very highest standard in superbly equipped state-of-the-art environments.

The Academies are committed to fostering good citizenship, self-reliance, and personal responsibility. Taking a central role within their communities, they share their facilities with other schools and the local neighborhood. They promote a broad, relevant and innovative curriculum with a special emphasis on one subject area. Capital City Academy will specialize in sports.

The new school, which replaced an outdated existing high school, takes the form of a long, gently curving linear building on the eastern edge of the site, close to the sports center. This form allows the perimeter of the site to be used for playing fields. The linear form produces a natural link between the historical entrance to the school and the sports center.

The school has been designed to provide flexible learning opportunities for its 1200 students and flexible teaching environments for 120 teachers, and can be reconfigured as teaching and learning styles develop in the future. In particular, the spacious internal street at the heart of the school, which contains informal research and study areas, promotes visual connections and interaction in a stable and safe environment. The street ramps gently along its length, responding to changes of level on the site.

The classrooms are large, with high ceilings. The partially glazed walls admit generous amounts of daylight and create visual links between classrooms and departments. Natural ventilation is used throughout.

Next to the main entrance is a hall, capable of seating 400 people, which will be used for assemblies, exhibitions, and performances. At the other end of the building is the dining hall, which overlooks the sunken sports hall.

Sustainable features:

✲ Natural cross ventilation ✲ Flexible learning environments for future adaptability ✲ Daylighting ✲ Optimized energy performance ✲ Theater, sports hall, library, and computer facilities made available to the community for after-hours use

1 Exterior view
2 Entrance
3 Exterior at night
4 Exterior detail

2

3

4

1

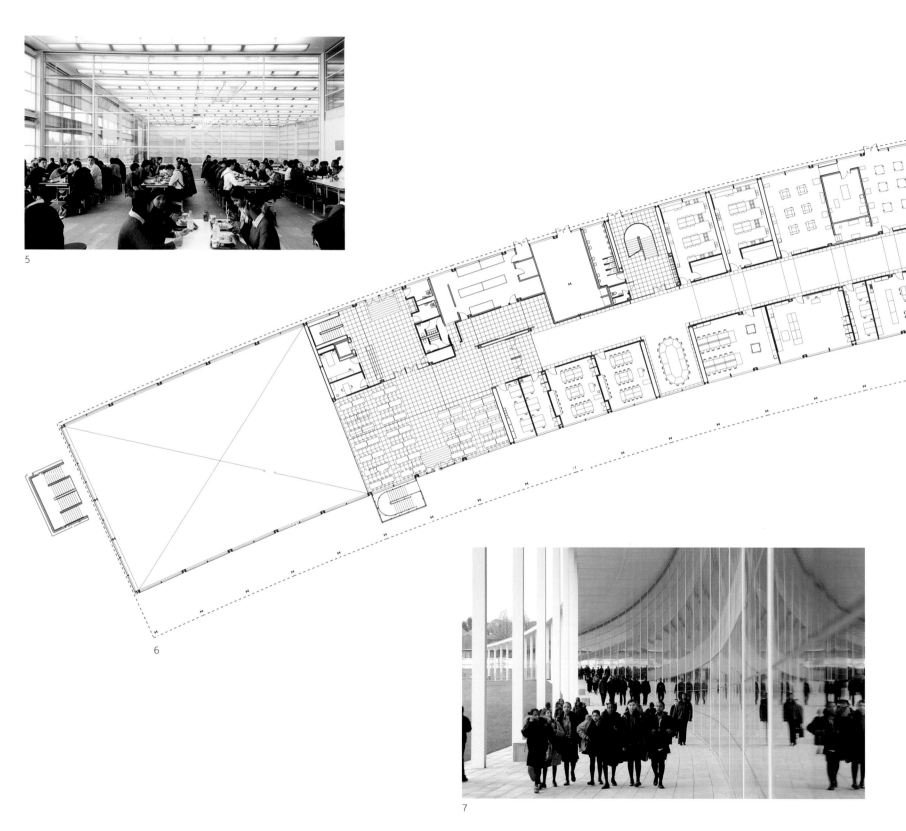

5

6

7

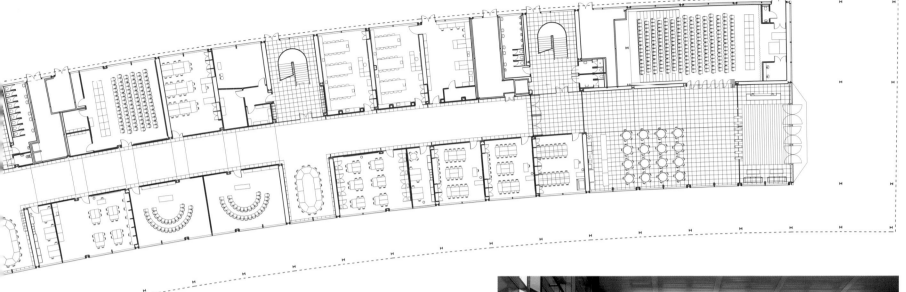

9

8

5   Dining hall

6   Floating ground floor plan

7   Building has a gently curved form

8   Interior central street

9   Interior view of entrance

10

11

12

10,11 Interior central street

12 Detail of interior central street showing bridges

13 Classroom

Photography: Nigel Young/Foster + Partners

13

Cesar Chavez Elementary School – Long Beach Unified School District

Long Beach, California, USA
LPA, Inc.

Sustainable features:

☼ East-west orientation reaps the greatest benefits from the sun and wind ☼ Natural ventilation systems are provided via operable clerestories, windows, and skylights ☼ Abundant natural daylight is provided from large operable north-facing windows, lightshelves, sunscreens, skylights, and rooftop light monitors ☼ Low-E laminated window glazing and a variety of shading features keep out sun heat and glare ☼ An automatic sensor system lowers and shuts down the indirect and direct T8 fluorescent lighting when sufficient daylighting is present ☼ A central water-cooled HVAC plant with fur-pipe fan coil units; operable skylights vent air from common areas; light monitors in the roof conduct heat out of the school ☼ Natural, recycled, and recyclable building materials are utilized throughout the project ☼ Landscaping, including abundant trees and light-colored concrete, reduces the heat island effect ☼ A green screen adds landscaping to the central quad and shades the outdoor lunch area

■ The concept for the Cesar Chavez Elementary School was to create a living laboratory to educate not only the students and faculty, but the local community as well. The school was also designed to be a catalyst in the revival of this downtown district, using architecture and landscape architecture to unite an adjacent residential neighborhood and business district.

The 75,000-square-foot (7000-square-meter), low-rise school is one of the first true "green" K-12 schools in California, and it was the first school in California to make use of Proposition 47's Energy Allowance Grant, a new state school facility grant program.

The campus has 34 classrooms, including a special education classroom, a multipurpose room that also serves as a gymnasium for the community after hours and on weekends, administration offices, a library, a computer learning center, and a separate kindergarten playground.

Whenever possible, environmental solutions were selected to prompt curiosity and strengthen the educational aspects of the design: an integrated central plant system is placed on an outside corner of the facility behind a perforated screen, providing a visible environmental solution; operable windows provide natural ventilation to 75 percent of the interior spaces; indigenous, drought-tolerant landscape provides shade to the integrated lunch shelter, which provides protection from the elements and abundant natural light.

Indirect lighting systems provide an obvious and effective solution. Daylight permeates 90 percent of the spaces, including the gymnasium and circulation corridors. Glass is protected from direct sun through the use of sun screens and shading devices. Energy usage and costs are reduced by 33 percent more than required by the California Title 24 energy code.

The school was planned holistically, responding to Collaborative for High Performance Schools (CHPS), LEED and Savings By Design requirements and has won design awards from Orange County AIA, South Bay AIA, Coalition for Adequate School Housing, Savings by Design, and the Concrete Masonry Institute.

1 View toward main entry

2 Site plan

3 South elevation

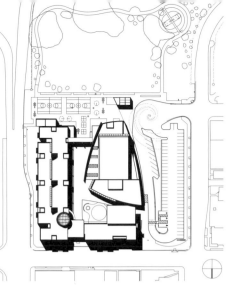

1

2

3

4

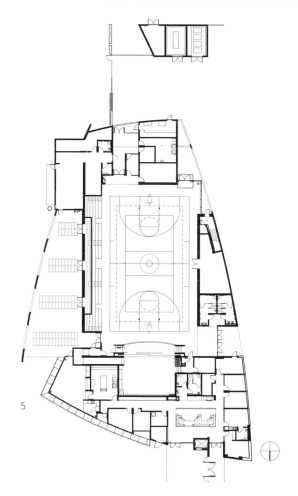

5

6

4   Courtyard/green screen

5   Floor plan

6   Playground

7,8   Courtyard detail

7

8

9 Operable clerestories and skylights diagram

10 Hallway/indirect lighting

11 Elevator shaft and main stair

12 Classroom

13 Light shelves and sunscreens diagram

Photography: Costea Photography

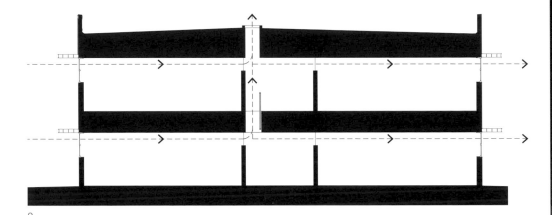

9

10

11

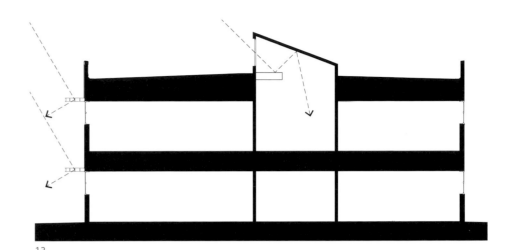

13

12

Chum Creek Outdoor Education Centre

Chum Creek, Victoria, Australia
FMSA Architects

Sustainable features:

✿ Thermal mass is incorporated through the use of polished concrete floors and mud brick walls ✿ Passive evaporative cooling is achieved by coupling water retention tanks with controlled through ventilation on the south side of the building ✿ Operable windows encourage cross-ventilation ✿ Ceiling fans redistribute rising heat to the lower areas of the spaces in winter and enhance cooling effects in summer ✿ Solar chimneys provide heated air in winter and induce cross-ventilation in summer ✿ Double-glazed windows reduce the rate of heat loss in winter ✿ Windows and substantial parts of the external walls are shaded by eaves and retractable awnings ✿ Building orientation to the north for best response to the microclimate ✿ Windows are limited on the south side of the building and maximized on the north side ✿ The building form deflects heavy winds from the south and southwest and shields the veranda and outdoor activity areas ✿ Site excavation works planned and managed to preserve natural habitats ✿ Building materials selected to avoid off-gassing and harmful by-products ✿ Wastewater is biologically treated using mini-ecosystems to produce a clean by-product used for irrigation ✿ Contractors required to demonstrate a commitment to sustainable practice, including management of site waste ✿ Rainwater tanks installed ✿ Evaporative cooling via a "wet wall" below the water tanks ✿ Darkened roofs enhance preheating of air supply to the solar chimneys

■ The learning program for this outdoor campus is called "earth education" and focuses on hands-on learning to assist students to understand the functioning of many environmental elements.

The design specifically incorporates sustainable building systems that require and invite user participation for their management. School students manipulate the building's heating, cooling, and ventilation systems by closing louvers, turning on the water drip system, opening windows, and pulling out awnings. These features demonstrate how, with intelligent design, natural systems can be controlled by simple physics and geometry.

The sculptural design introduces a new aesthetic for environmentally sustainable building. It references the Australian landscape and a typical bush "shelter" by the interplay of simple skillion roofs lying over external walls of corrugated iron cladding and recycled timber.

Energy efficiency and consumption are optimized through the adoption of adjustable systems that can be tuned to respond to suit daily and seasonal climatic changes for heating and cooling. The use of natural lighting is maximized and is complemented by high-efficiency artificial lighting. Draw-out awnings also act as light shelves to reflect daylight further into the space.

Intensive life cycle assessment of materials was undertaken, including minimizing embodied energy, maximizing durability of materials and, where possible, ensuring recyclability of the building fabric by designing demountable connections between materials. The building elements, where possible, were sized to reduce material wastage and selected to decrease toxicity and off-gassing. Recycled timber and macrocarpa reclaimed from farm windbreaks is featured in the veranda and wall claddings. Local suppliers and contractors were sourced to minimize transport.

Off-site disposal of waste is minimized by on-site treatment that includes composting and a worm farm that treats organic waste; a recycling programme has been instigated for plastic, glass, and compostables.

1 Façade detail: solar chimney and timber decks

2 Corner façade detail

3 Front façade

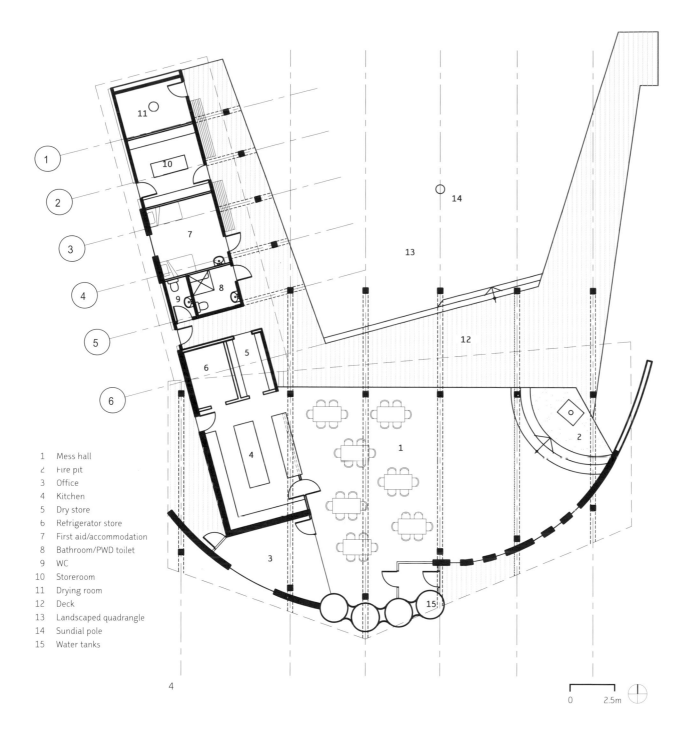

1   Mess hall
2   Fire pit
3   Office
4   Kitchen
5   Dry store
6   Refrigerator store
7   First aid/accommodation
8   Bathroom/PWD toilet
9   WC
10 Storeroom
11 Drying room
12 Deck
13 Landscaped quadrangle
14 Sundial pole
15 Water tanks

4

0   2.5m

5

6

4   Floor plan

5   View to mess hall and fire pit area

6   View of internally expressed corrugated metal rainwater tanks

Photography: Peter Clarke

Clackamas High School

Clackamas, Oregon, USA
BOORA Architects

Sustainable features:

✿East-west solar orientation ✿Light shelves and sunshades distribute light and limit solar gain ✿Faceted ceilings distribute light ✿Courtyard trees prevent solar gain heat in concrete and shade adjacent classrooms ✿Natural ventilation and cooling with temperature regulators in all classrooms, common areas, and gymnasiums via mechanically controlled dampers, louvers, and air stacks ✿Solatubes channel light from the second floor to the first floor ✿Materials such as sustainable natural linoleum, made primarily from sawdust and linseed oil ✿Recycled materials, such as plastic toilet partitions, rubber flooring, and upholstery ✿Concrete slabs and concrete masonry walls are used as thermal masses ✿Low-toxicity and low-E building materials ✿Integrated energy monitoring and control system allowed for substantial downsizing of the HVAC system ✿A small photovoltaic system has been installed, with provisions made for a future rooftop photovoltaic system ✿Covered bicycle parking area is pre-wired for a future photovoltaic system ✿Existing plants were cataloged, removed, and replanted on the site ✿Biofiltration in retention areas adjacent to nearby wetlands preserves the wetlands and incorporates a high percentage of native plants

■ Located in a growing residential neighborhood, Clackamas High School serves a student population of 1800 and is a center for continuing education, community meetings, and district-wide athletic activities.

The 265,355-square-foot (24,652-square-meter) building is divided into four two-story academic houses with a library/media center between them. A central commons/lobby area with administration and counseling services connects the fine and performing arts wing, the special education areas, support spaces, and physical education facilities. Small-scale learning environments emphasize flexibility, integration of instruction, technology, and spaces for social interaction and community use.

The design team integrated a total site and building energy analysis in the design process and established specific requirements for the building envelope, HVAC, lighting systems, materials, and landscaping features. Extensive daylighting lab and model studies were used to detail light modulation elements, and consideration of the students' relationship to natural light shaped the form and layout of the school. The team balanced capital costs for operating systems with life cycle and energy use analysis.

Cited by *The Green Guide* as the most sustainable school in the United States, Clackamas High School is oriented on an east-west axis for optimal daylighting, ventilation, and solar control. Windows, skylights, and light shelves provide daylight and views to 90 percent of occupied spaces. Natural ventilation and cooling is incorporated into all classrooms, common areas, and the gymnasium via mechanically controlled dampers, louvers, and air stacks. Concrete slabs and concrete masonry walls provide thermal mass to stabilize internal air temperatures throughout the year.

Automated occupancy, carbon dioxide, and lighting sensors ensure that artificial light and mechanical ventilation is provided only when needed, allowing for substantial downsizing of the HVAC system and contributing to an overall energy saving of 44 percent compared to conventionally designed buildings. Clackamas High School is LEED Silver certified.

1   A courtyard placed along an east-west axis allows greater daylighting and natural ventilation penetration of the building

2   Clear glass above the light shelves and tinted glass below maximize the available light reflected into classrooms in cooler months while reducing excess heat and glare during the summer

3   A detail of the entry clerestory

2

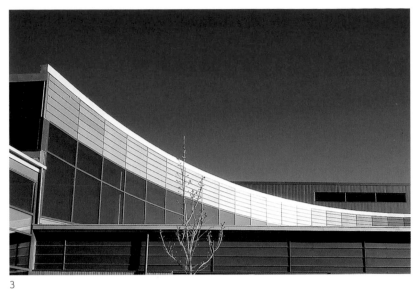

3

1

4

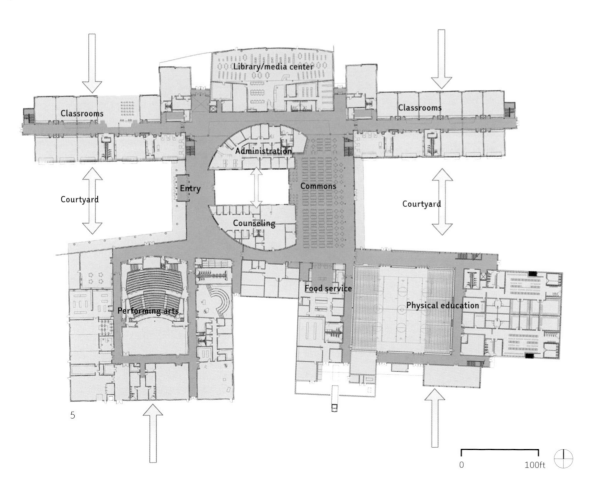

Library/media center

Classrooms

Administration

Entry

Courtyard

Commons

Counseling

Courtyard

Classrooms

Food service

Performing arts

Physical education

5

0   100ft

6

7

8

9

10

4 Skylights and angled ceilings allow complete daylighting of the upstairs hallway; ventilation shafts at the roof convect warm air out of the upper and lower floors of the building, in turn drawing fresh air into the building

5 First floor plan showing daylight entry via outdoor spaces along the east-west oriented building masses

6 The light shelves shade south-facing windows, which receive intense direct sunlight; natural ventilation louvers sit below the windows

7 Courtyards are placed along an east-west axis, allowing greater daylighting penetration into the building

8 A large curtain wall allows extensive daylight to enter the north-facing library

9 A typical daylit classroom with light shelves, sunshades, and faceted ceiling to bounce light deep into the space, while light interior tones distribute it evenly

10 The building's solar orientation allows clerestories in the entry to bring daylight into the space throughout the day

11 Building plan showing natural ventilation via exterior walls and outdoor spaces

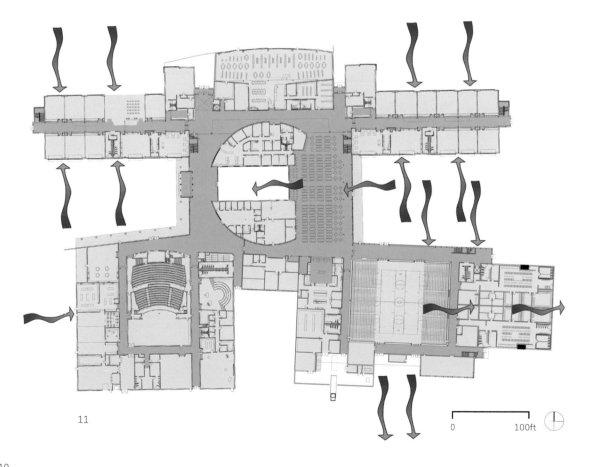

11

0   100ft

12 In the commons, slabs and concrete masonry walls are used as thermal masses to stabilize internal air temperatures throughout the year

13 Curtain walls and angled ceilings allow the cafeteria to use virtually no electric light

14 Skylights and faceted ceiling allow complete daylighting of the upstairs hallway

15 Solatubes, concealed within the banks of lockers, channel daylight from the second floor to the first floor

16 The gymnasium's displacement natural ventilation system

Photography: Michael Mathers for BOORA Architects

12

13

14

15

16

Cottage Lake Elementary School

Woodinville, Washington, USA
Bassetti Architects

A pilot project for the Washington State School Sustainability Protocol, Cottage Lake Elementary uses site orientation, extensive daylighting, natural ventilation, and a water infiltration system as strategies to reduce energy usage and increase occupant comfort. Separate buildings connected by covered walkways make up the campus, with a central amphitheater to accommodate performance and classroom activities in an outdoor setting.

The design incorporates 100 percent on-site stormwater infiltration. Impervious areas were reduced by 12 percent across the site by minimizing building footprint and paved areas. New biofiltration/infiltration zones and raingarden planters were created. The cost of this sustainable civil design was approximately 43 percent of a conventional stormwater conveyance system, and generated almost $100,000 in savings to the project.

A central, two-story shaft introduces daylight and passive ventilation into the building core. Enough natural lighting is provided to each learning space to eliminate the need for artificial lighting in most conditions. Other daylight controls include exterior sun shading devices, interior light shelves, skylights, and photocell dimming. Teachers find that turning off the lights provides a calmer classroom atmosphere and that daylight provides adequate light for critical tasks.

Thermo-dynamic modeling shows that convection ventilation has provided more cooling than a ducted mechanical system: all learning spaces are naturally cooled through ventilation. Natural cooling at Cottage Lake is achieved through operable windows and ceiling fans in every classroom. Cost benefits include a front-end $1.20 per square foot utility rebate, and an estimated $5000 in annual energy cost savings. Significant savings were achieved by eliminating fans, ducts, and chillers.

The Cottage Lake Elementary staff and community have an awareness of sustainability, which supported the design process. Raingardens, biofiltration, passive ventilation, and daylighting elements are all perceived as educational opportunities to deepen the school's academic program.

Sustainable features:

✿ 100% stormwater infiltration ✿ Creation of biofiltration/infiltration zones and raingarden planters ✿ Central two-story shaft for daylight and passive ventilation ✿ Artificial lighting eliminated in most conditions ✿ Exterior sunshades, interior light shelves, skylights, and photocell dimming control daylight ✿ Natural cooling achieved though operable windows and ceiling fans; fans, ducts, and chillers were eliminated

1   View of roof drainage and rain garden

2   Covered outdoor play area

3   Classroom building, north elevation

4   North face of the library building

5   Classroom building, south elevation

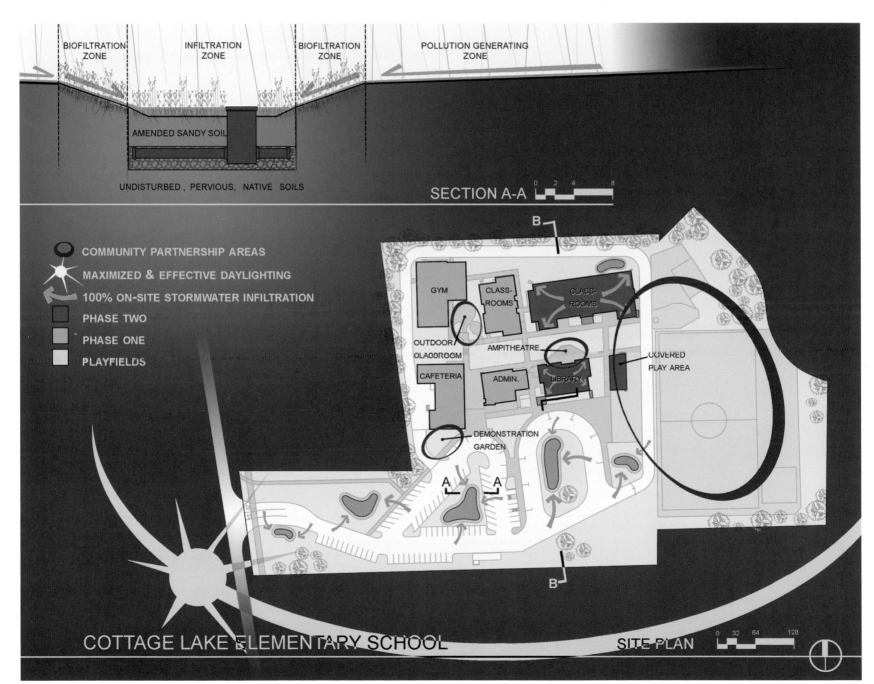

BIOFILTRATION ZONE   INFILTRATION ZONE   BIOFILTRATION ZONE   POLLUTION GENERATING ZONE

AMENDED SANDY SOIL

UNDISTURBED , PERVIOUS, NATIVE SOILS

SECTION A-A   0 2 4 8

COMMUNITY PARTNERSHIP AREAS

MAXIMIZED & EFFECTIVE DAYLIGHTING

100% ON-SITE STORMWATER INFILTRATION

PHASE TWO

PHASE ONE

PLAYFIELDS

B

GYM

CLASS-ROOMS

CLASS-ROOMS

OUTDOOR/ CLASSROOM

AMPITHEATRE

COVERED PLAY AREA

CAFETERIA

ADMIN.

LIBRARY

DEMONSTRATION GARDEN

A   A

B

COTTAGE LAKE ELEMENTARY SCHOOL   SITE PLAN   0 32 64 128

6

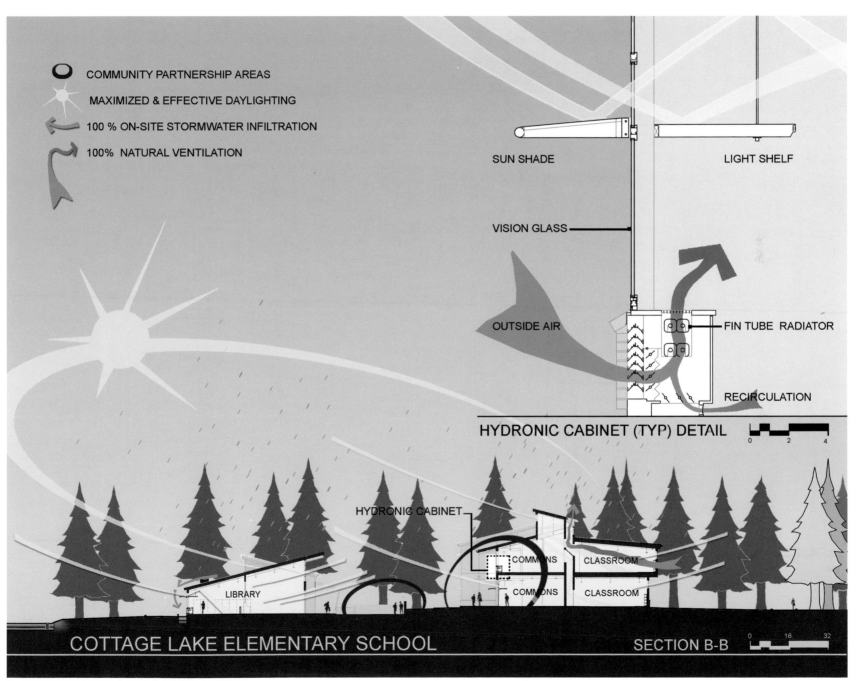

COMMUNITY PARTNERSHIP AREAS

MAXIMIZED & EFFECTIVE DAYLIGHTING

100 % ON-SITE STORMWATER INFILTRATION

100% NATURAL VENTILATION

SUN SHADE

LIGHT SHELF

VISION GLASS

OUTSIDE AIR

FIN TUBE RADIATOR

RECIRCULATION

HYDRONIC CABINET (TYP) DETAIL

0   2   4

HYDRONIC CABINET

COMMONS   CLASSROOM

COMMONS   CLASSROOM

LIBRARY

COTTAGE LAKE ELEMENTARY SCHOOL

SECTION B-B

0   16   32

7

8

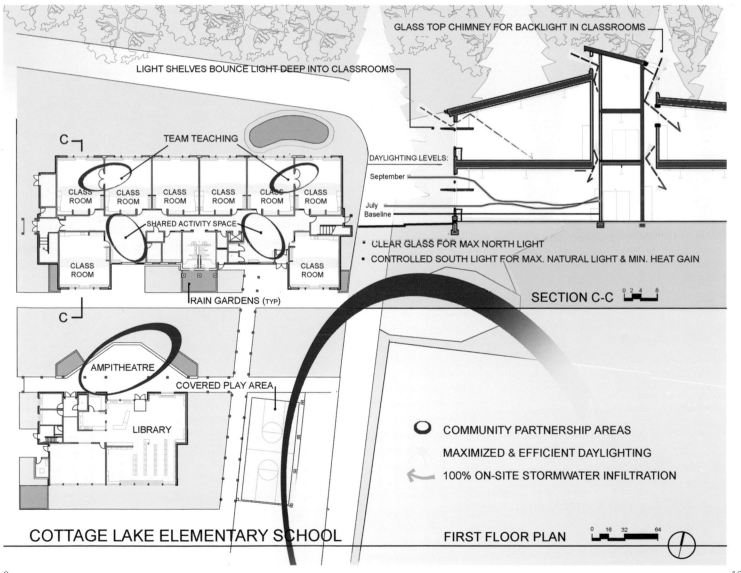

GLASS TOP CHIMNEY FOR BACKLIGHT IN CLASSROOMS

LIGHT SHELVES BOUNCE LIGHT DEEP INTO CLASSROOMS

TEAM TEACHING

CLASS ROOM | CLASS ROOM | CLASS ROOM | CLASS ROOM | CLASS ROOM | CLASS ROOM

SHARED ACTIVITY SPACE

CLASS ROOM

CLASS ROOM

RAIN GARDENS (TYP)

DAYLIGHTING LEVELS:

September

July
Baseline

- CLEAR GLASS FOR MAX NORTH LIGHT
- CONTROLLED SOUTH LIGHT FOR MAX. NATURAL LIGHT & MIN. HEAT GAIN

SECTION C-C   0 2 4 8

AMPITHEATRE

COVERED PLAY AREA

LIBRARY

○ COMMUNITY PARTNERSHIP AREAS

MAXIMIZED & EFFICIENT DAYLIGHTING

← 100% ON-SITE STORMWATER INFILTRATION

COTTAGE LAKE ELEMENTARY SCHOOL

FIRST FLOOR PLAN   0 16 32 64

9

10

8 Daylit classroom on lower floor

9 Classroom daylighting study

10 Hallways and shared activity areas have abundant natural light

11 Shared activity area

12 Library clerestory windows provide daylight without glare

Photography: Doug Scott Photography (1-5,11); courtesy Bassetti Architects (6,7,9); Dale Lang, Northwest Architectural Photography (8,10,12)

11

12

Discovery Canyon Campus

Colorado Springs, Colorado, USA
Antoine Predock Architect, PC

■ Discovery Canyon is a learning encounter between students, faculty, and visitors and the high plains topography of eastern Colorado Springs. A stream of events and phenomena choreograph a spontaneous journey of discovery, visually culminating in Pike's Peak.

In contrast to the typical separation of elementary, middle, and high school campuses, Discovery Canyon is a preschool through grade twelve public school contained within a single campus. This concept maximizes the desired vertical articulation and cross-pollination between grades. The curriculum components provide a strong focus on math and science with an emphasis on aeronautics and space exploration.

Technology meets ritual and is played out in real life in the journey from amphitheater and sport on the east to gardens, a fishpond/hatchery, and riparian habitat that merge with the school to the west. Major event venues, such as the theater and gymnasium, and primary contact points, including administration, create the south edge of the canyon. Views to Pike's Peak are always prioritized with foreground berms built from the canyon excavation.

The canyon concept allows for the incorporation of teaching courtyards, as well as maximum use of available daylight for interior spaces. As an abstraction of the landscape, the integral color of the masonry was selected to closely match that observed on site. The existing well-drained topsoil supports a variety of native grasses and scrub vegetation. This area of the Rocky Mountain Front Range can experience sporadic strong westerly winds, as well as potentially severe winter storms traveling down from the north. With its east-west orientation and threshold components of cross circulation, the Discovery Canyon design mitigates the severity of weather experienced on the site.

Wherever possible, classrooms expand outdoors to adjacent terraces for playing, eating, or experimenting. The architecture of the school is malleable and kinetic in response to changing environmental conditions and seasons.

Sustainable features:

✧ Orientation of building volumes with regard to environmental exposure ✧ Protection from environment (wind, sun, snow) ✧ Shading of large glazed areas exposed to harsh sun angles
✧ Separation of building volumes allows for maximum natural daylight into classroom area ✧ Vinyl composition tile is 90% limestone, a sustainable material

1 View from wetlands

2 View from spiral plaza and talus to upper plaza

3 Spiral plaza and chalkboard wall

2

3

1

4 Art bridge crossing Discovery Canyon Campus links public and administrative areas

5 Aerial view looking toward Rocky Mountains

6 Level 1 floor plan

7 Level 3 floor plan

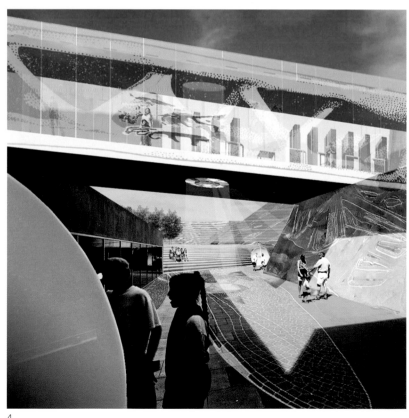

4

5

Level 1

1 Elementary school physical education
2 Elementary school cafeteria/multipurpose
3 Restroom
4 Elementary school administration
5 Elementary school special education suite
6 Elementary school classroom
7 Elementary school multi-use
8 Elementary school music performance
9 Elementary school art

Level 3

1 Entry
2 Middle school gymnasium
3 Middle school girls' locker room
4 Middle school boys' locker room
5 Middle school gymnasium storage
6 Middle school gymnasium office
7 High school classroom
8 High school specialty classroom
9 High school multi-use classroom
10 High school classroom storage
11 Restroom
12 High school special education classroom
13 High school special education itinerant space
14 High school special education kitchen/prep/laundry
15 High school special education storage
16 High/middle school cafeteria multi-use room
17 Middle school kitchen
18 Middle school special programs storage
19 Middle school science lab
20 Middle school classroom
21 Hybrid classroom
22 Middle school team office
23 Middle school storage
24 Middle school support
25 Middle school technology lab
26 Middle school technical education
27 Middle school foreign language
28 High/middle/elementary school lounge
29 Middle school principal
30 Middle school department office
31 Middle school conference
32 Middle school workroom/storage
33 Middle school record storage
34 Middle school reception
35 High school reception
36 High school conference
37 High school counsellor
38 High school career center
39 High school conference and testing
40 High school storage
41 High school department office
42 High school work room
43 High school mail room
44 High school secretary
45 Community conference/seminar room
46 High school principal
47 Office storage

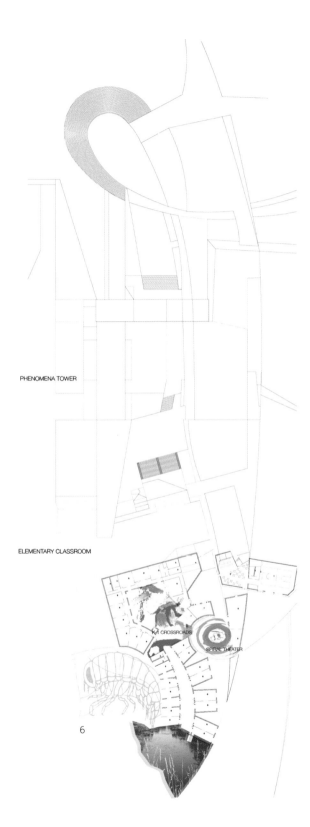

PHENOMENA TOWER

ELEMENTARY CLASSROOM

K–1 CROSSROADS

SPIRAL THEATER

6

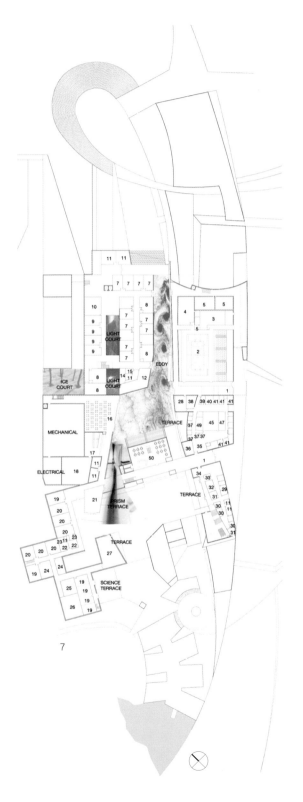

7

8   View of entry with Rocky Mountains in distance

9   Interior corridor with view to talus slope

10 Gymnasium wall with glass brick inserts

11 "Free-standing wall" illusion: same rock at base and on roof

12 Gymnasium interior with glass brick inserts

Photography: Stuart Blakely, Antoine Predock Architect, PC (1); Jon Hostager, M+O+A Architectural Partnership (3,8,10-12)

Renderings: courtesy Antoine Predock Architects, PC

8

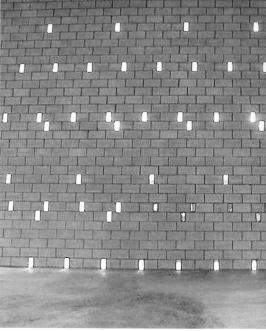

10

9

11

12

Druk White Lotus School

Ladakh, India
Arup Associates

■ The Druk White Lotus School is an entirely sustainable project. In its fragile ecological context, the site strategy aims to ensure a completely self-regulating system of water, energy, and waste management.

Locally available traditional materials are used: stone, mud mortar, mud bricks, timber, and grass. The stone is found on site and the mud for mortar, bricks, and roofing is excavated nearby. Poplar and willow timber are from nearby monastery plantations and local producers.

All buildings have cavity walls on three sides. Granite blocks set in mud mortar are used for the outer leaf, while traditional mudbrick masonry is used for the inner leaf, giving increased thermal performance and durability. The Ladakhi-style heavy mud roof is supported by a timber structure that is independent of the walls. Steel connections and cross bracings provide earthquake stability in this highly seismic zone.

Residential buildings use Trombe walls for passive solar heating. The walls are coated externally with heat-absorbing material and are faced with a double layer of glass. Heat passing through the glass is absorbed by the dark surface, stored in the wall, and conducted slowly inward through the masonry. Adjustable openings on the top and bottom of the thermal storage wall allow heat transfer from the air cavity to the room inside. In summer the Trombe walls are shaded and ventilated to prevent overheating, while the operable windows allow cross-ventilation, cooling, and fresh air.

Solar-powered pumps deliver potable ground water and irrigation water by gravity feed. Solar panels are used to charge batteries when the pumps are not operating. The electricity generated can be used for lighting or small power supply to the school buildings.

Traditional dry latrines have been enhanced to VIP (Ventilated Improved Pit) latrines. A double chamber system with an integrated solar-driven flue allows their operation as composting toilets and produces humus that can be used as fertilizer.

Sustainable features:

☼ Locally available materials used where possible ☼ Buildings incorporate natural ventilation, natural daylight, and passive solar heating ☼ Buildings oriented to exploit solar potential ☼ Energy use and emissions minimized ☼ Water use minimized ☼ Solar power used for water pumps and VIP latrines ☼ Excess power generated by solar panels used elsewhere for lighting or as a small power supply to the school buildings ☼ Trombe walls store heat and are used for passive solar heating ☼ Humus from composing toilets used as fertilizer

1   Nursery infants' courtyard from south

2   Residential courtyard from south

3   Master plan referencing junior school plan

2

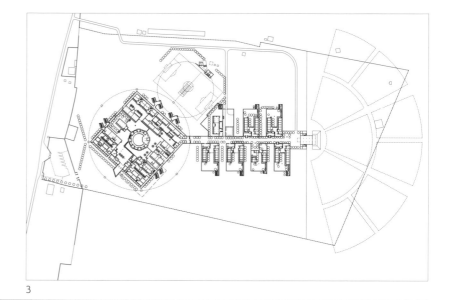

3

1

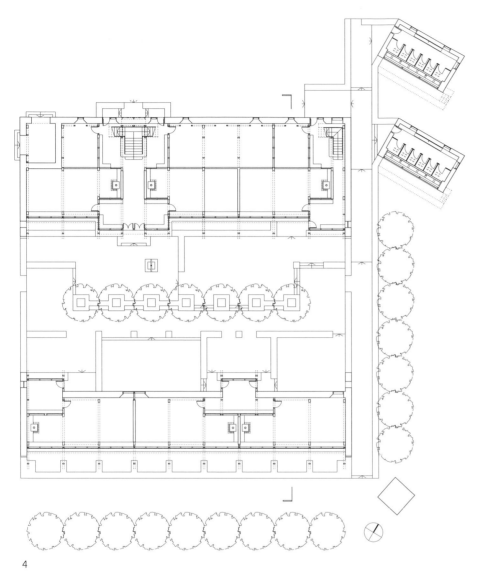

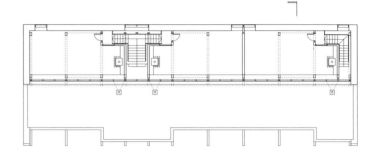

4

5

6

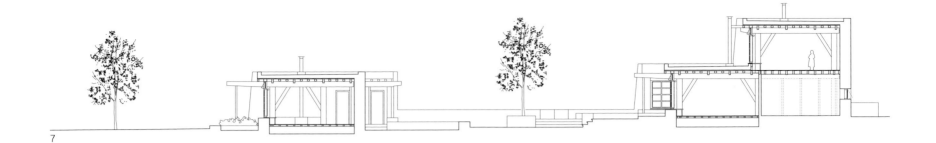

7

4 Plan of junior school

5 Granite wall with timber-framed window

6 Painting eaves during construction work

7 Section through junior school

8 View into infants' school courtyard

9 View of high-level windows in mountainous setting

8

9

10

11

12

10   Children resting in nursery classroom

11   South-facing glazing to nursery courtyard

12   High-level glazing and southern façade to nursery classroom

13   Interior view of nursery butterfly roof

14   Nursery school children in classroom

15   Infants' class in progress

Photography: Caroline Sohie

13

15

14

Eagle Rock Elementary School

Eagle Point, Oregon, USA
Dull Olson Weekes Architects

■ Located in southern Oregon, 10 miles (16 kilometers) from Medford, Eagle Point has just 5000 residents. Once surrounded by thriving lumber mills, the community has experienced lean years as the timber industry has declined.

Despite these hardships, residents passed a bond issue to build a new elementary school. The 394-student grade school, Eagle Rock Elementary (kindergarten through fifth grade), is a 38,850-square-foot (3610-square-meter) $7-million school that opened in November 2003. The school comprises numerous sustainable features.

Dull Olson Weekes Architects designed Eagle Rock Elementary to save an estimated 38 percent more energy than a building constructed to Oregon building codes.

The school uses daylighting extensively. Sunshades are installed on the outside of the south side of the building to prevent excessive heat gain. The gym and corridor systems have skylights that allow ample daylight and eliminate the need for artificial lighting on many days. Classrooms are equipped with fluorescent lighting fixtures with T-5 lamps and energy-efficient ballasts. All have occupancy sensors that are estimated to reduce lighting usage by 30 percent.

The incorporation of multi-use spaces reduced the building size. The music room can be used as a community room; the cafeteria converts to a stage, and the gym to an assembly area; three special education rooms can be opened to make one big room for larger group presentations and after-school use. The gym, cafeteria, and community room have separate entrances so they can be opened for evening and weekend events without accessing or requiring operations of other parts of the building.

Sustainable features:

✿ Classroom windows are operable, allowing for natural ventilation ✿ Two central, natural gas-fired boilers heat water for the school; they have thermal efficiencies of 88% compared to the code standard efficiency of 80% ✿ Most waste generated during construction was recycled ✿ Low- or no-VOC paints, varnishes, adhesives used ✿ Existing vegetation was maintained where possible; drought-resistant species were selected elsewhere ✿ Water is stored and pre-cooled in three underground tanks before it goes to the chiller, reducing chiller use ✿ A bioswale and pond system in the hillside behind the school holds and filters rain run-off before it is discharged into a wetland area ✿ Bicycle parking area and access system of paths to surrounding residential areas; an estimated 95% of children walk or ride bikes to school ✿ The school "envelope" exceeds insulation requirements; a portion of the building is built into the hillside, relying on the earth for thermal insulation ✿ Low-flow plumbing fixtures; timed water faucets that turn off automatically ✿ Building was designed to minimize grading impacts, retain existing trees, and maintain wetlands that surround the site

1

1 Exterior view of learning center with natural landscaping and stormwater stream

2 Site plan

3 Community facility, Meet & Greet, and learning center

4 Exterior view of learning center

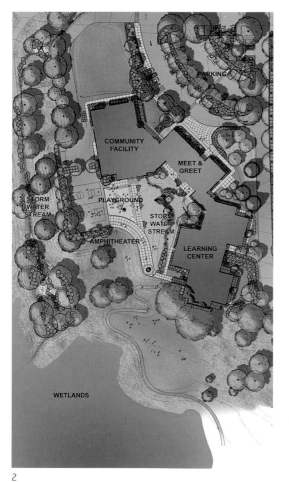

PARKING

COMMUNITY FACILITY

MEET & GREET

STORM WATER STREAM

PLAYGROUND

STORM WATER STREAM

AMPHITHEATER

LEARNING CENTER

WETLANDS

2

3

4

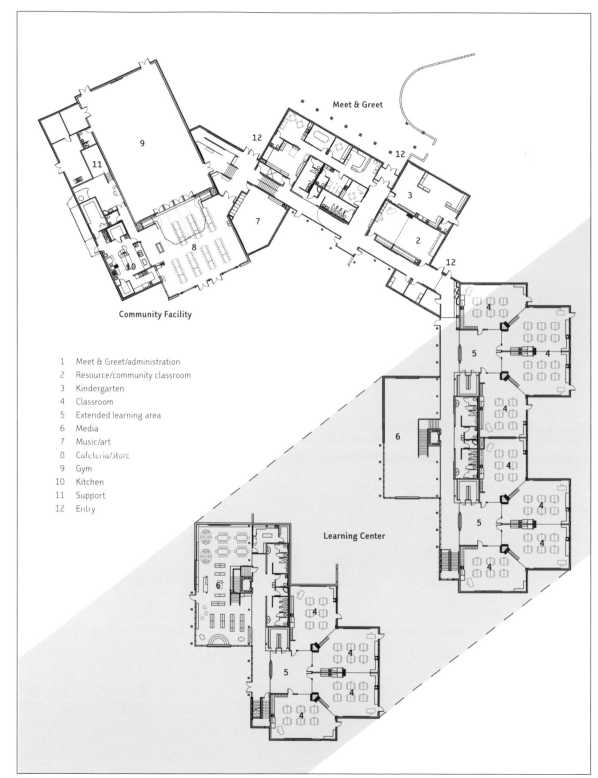

Meet & Greet

Community Facility

12

12

12

9

11

8

7

3

2

12

5

4

4

4

4

6

4

4

5

Learning Center

6

4

5

4

4

1 Meet & Greet/administration
2 Resource/community classroom
3 Kindergarten
4 Classroom
5 Extended learning area
6 Media
7 Music/art
8 Cafeteria/store
9 Gym
10 Kitchen
11 Support
12 Entry

6

5

7

Photography: Gary Wilson Photo/Graphic (1-4,8, 11,12);
courtesy Dull Olson Weekes Architects (6,7,10)

9

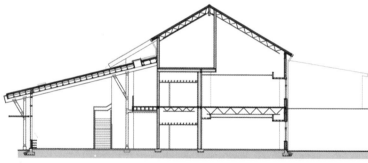

10

11

12

Ebenezer Trust School Campus and Orphanage

Livingstone, Zambia
Studio B Architects

■ This project entails master planning a multi-stage campus plan for the Ebenezer Trust School and Orphanage. Phase 1 of the project will provide educational facilities for 250 students and on-site housing for 50 children, primary school, secondary school, administration, science laboratory, assembly hall, medical clinic, craft training center, security, and employee housing. The final completed master plan will educate more than 600 Zambian children, including 75 orphans living on site.

Locally available building materials and labor will be used where possible. Many of the exterior walls will be composed of burnt brick, a termite-resistant material with thermal properties, easy availability, and no harmful toxins. Steel will be used as the major structural element in most of the buildings; sustainably harvested wood will be used for secondary structural elements. Roofing materials will consist of thatch, metal, and corrugated acrylic. Locally woven fabrics and textiles and other commonly occurring materials have been incorporated into the design.

Gray water collection systems have been designed so that water can be collected in sealed cisterns to be used for gardens or other non-potable water needs. Composting toilets will be used and a solar water heater will provide most of the hot water requirements.

All buildings are surrounded by a usable covered space for gathering, entry, and other outdoor activities. These spaces draw breezes, creating a cool and pleasant environment under the protection of the roof. Roof insulation will prevent overheating on summer days and over-cooling on winter nights.

The buildings have an open clerestory level, providing fresh air and a high level of indoor air quality. Insect screens in wooden frames will be installed at every clerestory opening. Skylights are used to provide better daylighting to interior spaces, not only reducing the quantity of lights needed, but significantly reducing usage time and increasing lighting quality. High-efficiency electronic fluorescent fittings should be used throughout the complex.

Many buildings in the campus benefit from being orientated on an east–west axis. Long extending roofs and eaves cool the interior and exterior spaces beneath them. Trees and large overhangs protect the western walls from the hot-season afternoon sun.

Sustainable features:

✿ Natural day lighting ✿ Green materials ✿ Low-maintenance materials ✿ High-performance glazing ✿ Passive and active solar design ✿ Passive cooling and heating ✿ Composting toilets ✿ Solar water heating ✿ Natural daylighting in all classrooms ✿ Access to views and outdoor spaces ✿ Gray water recycling ✿ High indoor air quality

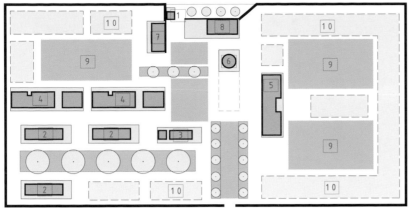

1	Security hut	5	Laboratory	9	Sports field
2	Orphan housing	6	Assembly hall	10	Future buildings
3	Director's house	7	Medical clinic		
4	Classroom unit	8	Training center		

1

3

1 Site plan

2 Aerial view of campus and main entry

3 View of assembly hall with operable chalkboard and textile panels

4 Perspective view of primary school buildings and courtyard

2

4

5 Classroom building section

6 North-south section of classroom building

7 Plan of classroom building

8 North elevation of a typical classroom building

1 Water collection
2 Classroom
3 Terrace

5

6

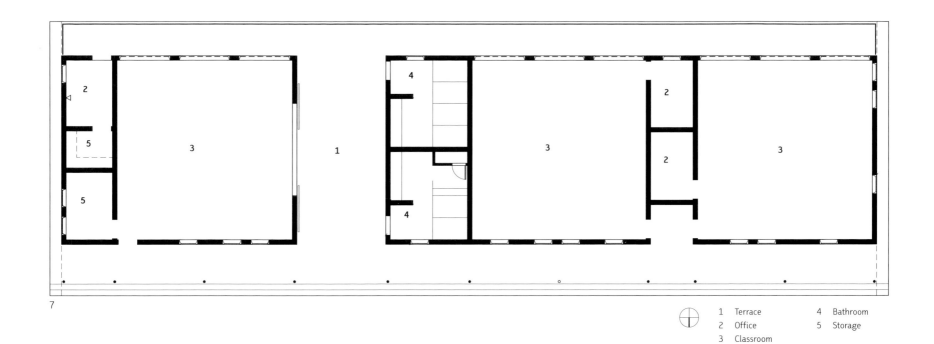

7

1 Terrace   4 Bathroom
2 Office   5 Storage
3 Classroom

8

9 Plan of orphan housing building

10 Covered breezeway of school director's housing

11 Perspective view of craft training center

12 Laboratory building sections

13 Sectional view of science laboratory building and breezeway

Renderings: courtesy Studio B Architects

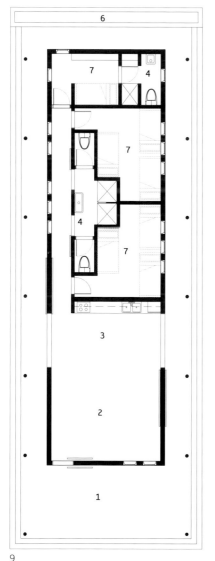

1   Terrace
2   Living
3   Kitchen
4   Bathroom
5   Storage
6   Water collection
7   Bedroom

9

10

11

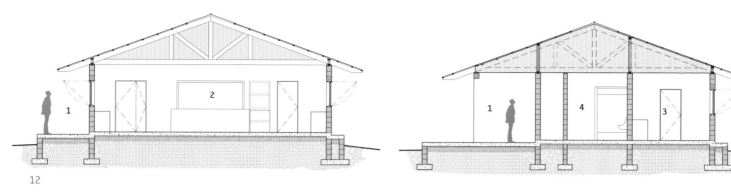

12

1 Terrace
2 Science lab
3 Science prep
4 Bathroom

13

Esther Eastman Music Center, Hotchkiss School

Lakeville, Connecticut, USA
Jefferson B. Riley, FAIA of Centerbrook Architects and Planners

Sustainable features:

⚙ Includes bicycle storage and changing rooms for occupants ⚙ Achieves almost 40% efficiency rating over ASHRAE 90.1 baseline ⚙ Zero CFC-based refrigerants in HVAC system ⚙ High-efficiency central chiller plant optimizes building operation times and reduces energy consumption ⚙ VFDs installed on supply and return fans to modulate speeds (during occupied hours) based on temperature and carbon dioxide ⚙ Setback mode in the music pavilion allows the fan to operate, louvers in roof to open and provide natural ventilation when pavilion doors and windows are open ⚙ Green power usage: electricity purchased from New York State wind farm ⚙ Occupancy sensors in all rooms ⚙ High-efficiency lighting ⚙ Uses materials with recycled content: structural steel and copper for wall and roof panels ⚙ Uses locally manufactured building materials ⚙ Includes rapidly renewable materials: bamboo flooring and linoleum counters ⚙ CO2 monitoring system ⚙ Adopts an IAQ management plan during construction ⚙ Low-VOC paints, coatings, and sealants ⚙ Includes carpet with high recycled content and low-VOC adhesives

■ The initial charge from the Hotchkiss School was to design an addition to the Walker Auditorium wing of the school's main building to house rehearsal halls, practice rooms, and classrooms for a rejuvenated music arts program. Performances, it was assumed, would take place in the auditorium's 650-seat theater.

Upon study, it was determined that the existing theater, while an excellent venue for drama, was ill-suited acoustically and configurationally for orchestral, instrumental, or choral performances. Centerbrook argued that the resources needed to remedy the old theater be redirected to create a new performance hall for music that could also fulfill the need for rehearsal space and for other school events and functions as well.

A major consideration in the design of the new building was to embrace the panoramic view of distant lake and hills that is a major asset of the campus. Additionally, Hotchkiss wanted the new building to exemplify its growing commitment to environmental responsibility.

The Esther Eastman Music Center unites the music arts and theater arts at Hotchkiss. The centerpiece of the music center is Katherine M. Elfers Hall, a glass-walled 715-seat music pavilion. The music center also includes classrooms, individual and ensemble practice rooms, a music technology studio, a radio station, and faculty offices.

The all-glass music pavilion provides dramatic views of the Berkshires. The pavilion's glass walls are 1¼-inch thick (31 millimeter) insulated, low-E, high-performance acoustic glazing panels. They provide excellent acoustic and insulating properties and are faceted at two levels to diffract sound to produce a full, clear tone.

Seating in the pavilion is configured in the round with parterre and upper-level balconies surrounding a flat-floor orchestra. Adjustable acoustic drapes, housed above suspended sound-reflecting panels, give the pavilion flexibility in accommodating a wide range of musical instruments and performances. Double doors at grade expand the pavilion to a terrace and lawn for summer concerts open to the community.

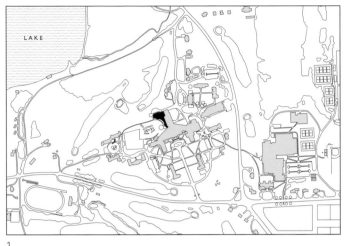

1 Campus plan

2 Detail of glass façade in Katherine M. Elfers Hall

3 The music pavilion opens to the panorama of the Berkshires

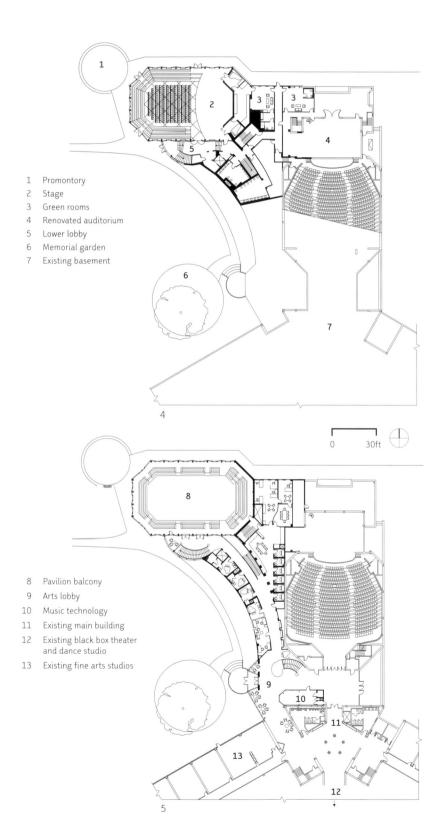

1 Promontory
2 Stage
3 Green rooms
4 Renovated auditorium
5 Lower lobby
6 Memorial garden
7 Existing basement

4

0   30ft

8 Pavilion balcony
9 Arts lobby
10 Music technology
11 Existing main building
12 Existing black box theater and dance studio
13 Existing fine arts studios

5

4   Lower entrance–stage level plan

5   Main entrance–balcony level plan

6   Katherine M. Elfers Hall

7   Detail of Katherine M. Elfers Hall

Opposite:
    Performance in Katherine M. Elfers Hall

6

7

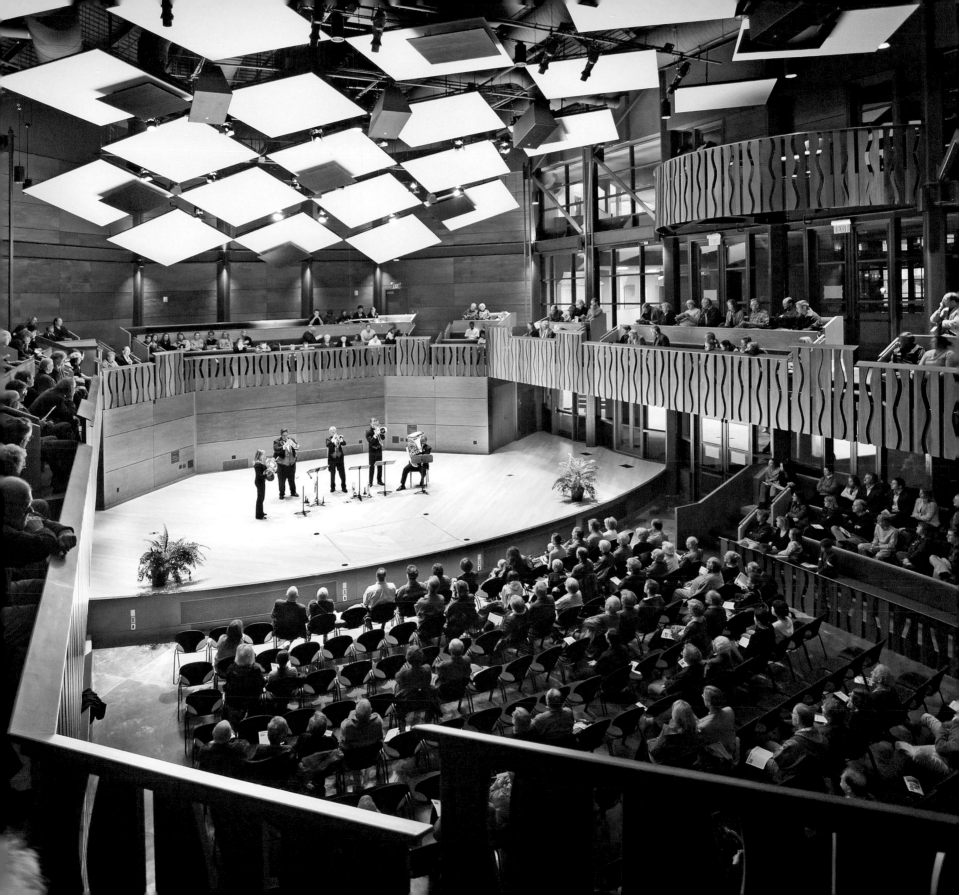

The design includes a sediment- and erosion-control plan specific to the site, water efficient landscaping, and a central chiller plant that optimizes building operation times. Sustainable materials and resources such as recycled structural steel and recycled copper wall and roof panels were used. The music center is expected to receive LEED certified status in 2007.

9   Upper level lounge

10   Main corridor and staircase with natural light provided by skylights

11   Main lobby

12   Ensemble room lit by skylight

Photography: Peter Aaron/Esto

9

10

11

12

Fossil Ridge High School

Fort Collins, Colorado, USA
RB+B Architects, Inc.

■ Fossil Ridge High School (FRHS) is the third high school in the United States to attain LEED Silver certification. RB+B Architects led an integrated design team that included recognized leaders in green building, and worked closely with the Poudre School District, the City of Fort Collins Utilities, and the Institute for the Built Environment at Colorado State University. FRHS was built in the same price range as a conventional high school and incorporates innovative technologies that will provide long-term benefits to the community, the environment, and the economic condition of the school district.

The school is composed of three learning communities of 600 students each, with internal administration and student services. Flexibility in the program is demonstrated by features such as retractable seating in the auditorium, which creates additional fine arts instruction space; an indoor running track, which is incorporated through the main and auxiliary gymnasiums; and sharing of the culinary arts and career and technical education programs with the local community college.

Fossil Ridge High School earned the highest design awards from both AASA (American Association of School Administrators) and CEFPI (Council of Educational Facility Planners International).

Sustainable features:

☼ Approximately 60% of required lighting levels are achieved from controlled daylight ☼ Electrical energy purchased is 100% wind-produced ☼ Thermal ice storage cooling ☼ First year utility estimated savings of $105,000 over previously built high school of the same size ☼ Recycled and low-VOC materials used throughout ☼ Xeriscaping and bioswales provided for water conservation and water quality

1

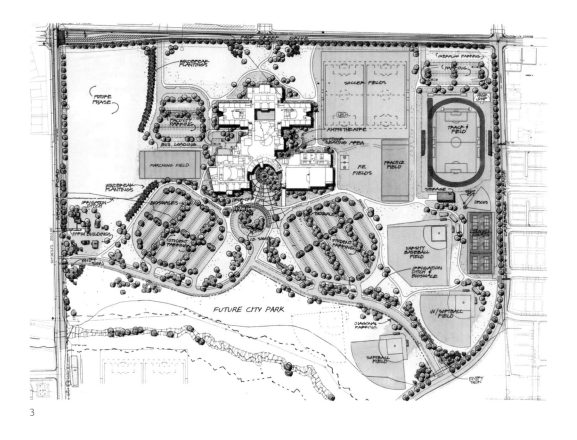

3

2

4

1　PV panel sunshades demonstrate the district's commitment to energy savings

2　Shaded high classroom windows with view windows below balance light and energy

3　Site plan with city parkland to the south

4　Three separate entries (auditorium, main, athletic) flank the entry courtyard

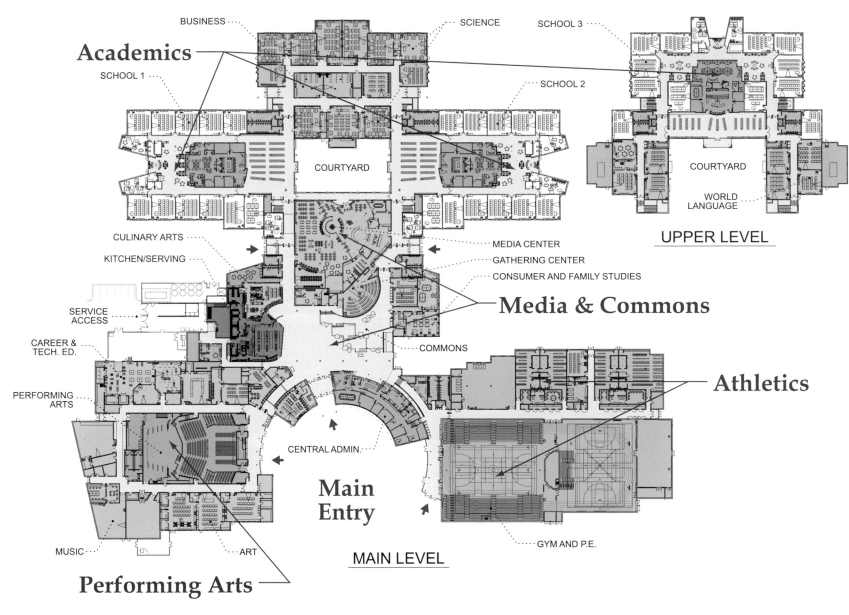

Academics

BUSINESS

SCIENCE

SCHOOL 3

SCHOOL 1

SCHOOL 2

COURTYARD

COURTYARD

UPPER LEVEL

WORLD LANGUAGE

CULINARY ARTS

KITCHEN/SERVING

MEDIA CENTER

GATHERING CENTER

CONSUMER AND FAMILY STUDIES

Media & Commons

SERVICE ACCESS

CAREER & TECH. ED.

COMMONS

Athletics

PERFORMING ARTS

CENTRAL ADMIN.

Main Entry

MUSIC

ART

GYM AND P.E.

MAIN LEVEL

Performing Arts

5

6

7　Classroom interior showing windows and direct/indirect photocell-controlled lighting

8　Daylit commons space is a joy to be in

9　Auditorium with upper-level retractable seating to the left

Photography: courtesy RB+B Architects

7

8

9

Francis Parker School

San Diego, California, USA
Lake|Flato Architects

The client requested a practical campus that captured its character and spirit, centered on the student experience, improved educational opportunities, and took advantage of San Diego's benevolent climate. The school was founded 90 years ago on the principle that engaging the environment increased student awareness of the world and their place within it. The new upper school campus picks up on that spirit. Lake|Flato created a series of outdoor rooms, structures and transition spaces between the two that are tactile and modern, environmentally responsible and authentic, artful and engineered. Great public rooms, the quads, and lawns all become social spaces for the campus. Classroom walls slide into pockets, directly linking the spaces to the outdoors and bathing them in filtered natural light.

The new master plan re-envisions the school as a garden campus and a campus of gardens. It creates four new communal spaces: an upper school quad, a middle school quad, the Lancer Lawn, and an arts court, which have become the focal points for student interaction. Augmenting these large spaces are a series of smaller garden spaces that create intimate settings for additional interactions—a memorial garden, science experiment courts, native plant learning gardens, overlooks, and nature paths. The whole design imagines a new campus where outdoor spaces contribute equally to the learning environment.

The buildings will be models for creative sustainability. They incorporate tilt-up concrete walls that utilize high fly-ash content concrete and are animated by recycled glass. The wood façades on many of the buildings are constructed using sustainably forested redwood siding that provides visual warmth as well as the promise of longevity. All classrooms are naturally daylit with an innovative arrangement of highly tuned light shelves and sun shades that filter and direct breezes and sunlight.

The project has been divided into a series of three phases:

Phase I: Upper school classrooms, science center, commons and upper school quad

Phase II: Middle school classrooms, library, Lancer Lawn, commons and middle school quad

Phase III: Performing arts, visual arts, administration, student leadership, arts court

Sustainable features:

⚙ New buildings outperform state Title 24 energy targets by 32% ⚙ 1000-square-foot (93-square-meter) photovoltaic array on the roof of the science center ⚙ Natural ventilation of classrooms (designed to not need air conditioning) ⚙ Buildings oriented to capture prevailing breezes ⚙ Light shelves and sunshades to direct natural daylighting into spaces and reject heat ⚙ High-performance building envelopes ⚙ Maximum use of exterior spaces—for circulation, locker areas, courtyards, and pocketing glass doors that allow walls of buildings to disappear ⚙ Use of durable building materials, such as concrete and naturally weathering redwood siding ⚙ Use of sustainable products, including sustainably forested redwood, recycled glass used in canopies and as wall surface treatment, high fly-ash content concrete ⚙ Landscaping that uses drought-tolerant and native species

1 View of upper school classrooms from upper school quad

2 Copper soffit panels along the first-floor arcade of the upper school classrooms

3 Site plan

2

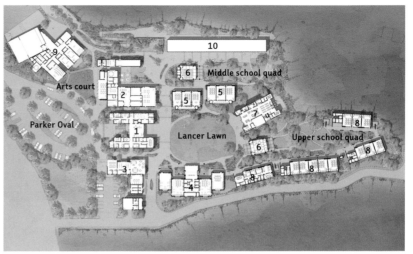

3

1	Administration	6	Commons
2	Visual arts	7	Library
3	Student leadership	8	Upper school
4	Science	9	Performing arts
5	Middle school	10	Existing middle school

1

4   Watercolor rendering of view from upper school quad toward upper school commons and classrooms

5   Watercolor rendering of view from upper school commons toward upper school quad

6   Recycled glass canopy for the upper school science building

7   Classroom section diagram depicting lightshelves that filter direct breezes and sunlight

8   Second-floor balconies overlooking upper school quad and campus beyond

Photography: Hewitt Garrison Architectural Photography
Renderings: Elizabeth Day

4

5

6

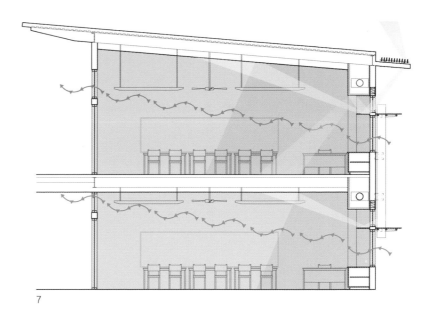

7

8

Hakuou High School

Miyagi Prefecture, Japan
Kazuhiro Kojima + Mitsumasa Sampei + Kazuko Akamatsu/C+A

■ The site is in a rural area, two hours from Tokyo by super express train. An agricultural high school and another high school, both with long traditions, were integrated and reincarnated as this larger high school. A varied educational program meets students' different interests and provides prerequisites for courses they may take in the future. The six main educational programs offered by the school are international/humanities studies, natural science, welfare education, information science, engineering, and agribusiness. Students can select courses from across the different programs, allowing them to independently organize their curriculums.

Compulsory subjects are mostly required for first-year students. At the second- and third-year levels, the number of elective/practical subjects increases. The students frequently move between classrooms, resulting in movement patterns that differ from those at other high schools.

To meet this highly specific program, the architects designed a square-shaped school building, and a "FLA" (flexible learning area) space. The FLA will be used as the students' main circulation space as well as a place where each student can communicate and mingle with students from all other courses. The architects called these multi-use spaces "white" spaces, distinguishing them from "black" spaces, which are purpose-built to accommodate their specific use. FLAs are also used for private study by students, and for meetings and small group seminars.

The solar panels installed onto the large square roof made it possible to reduce the running cost of the heating system for the FLA, therefore allowing student activities to continue throughout severe winter seasons.

Sustainable features:

✿ Extensive top daylighting throughout the school ✿ Classroom daylit from two sides ✿ Vertical and horizontal louvers for daylighting control ✿ Passive solar rooftop system utilized to heat the school ✿ Structural precast and prestressed concrete used to create flexible, column-free spaces to allow adaptability for changing academic needs ✿ Long lasting, durable materials used for interior and exterior surfaces

1

2

1　Aerial view

2　Overall view from the east

3　Inner courtyard

4　West side main entrance

3

4

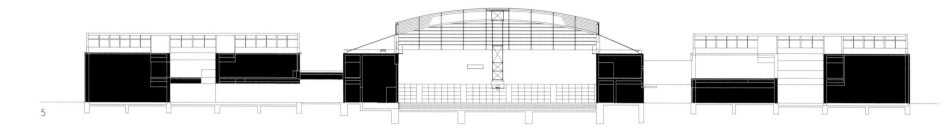

5

6

7

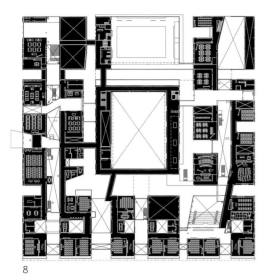

8

10

9

5   Section

6   Gymnasium

7   FLA (flexible learning area)

8   Floor plan

9   Corridor outside classrooms

10 Classroom

Photography: Hiroyuki Hirai

Hector Garcia Middle School

Dallas, Texas, USA
Perkins+Will

■ Hector Garcia Middle School, one of three new middle schools in the Dallas Independent School District's 2002 Bond Program, provides a broad selection of learning opportunities and services planned to meet the developmental needs of the whole child.

The new 175,000-square-foot (16,258-square-meter) school, serving 1200 students spanning grades six though eight, is organized around three teams per grade level. The design includes academic and support spaces to support classroom instruction, sciences, technology, and world languages for traditional, interdisciplinary, and project-based instruction. A special education program is centrally located to allow special needs students to be included in the social life of the school. Supporting and encouraging practical lifelong skills, the school offers flexible and technology enabled learning environments for career investigation, business education, and family consumer sciences.

The building's layout nurtures social and academic development in a safe and secure environment. Supporting the neighborhood and community beyond school hours, the building is zoned to allow public access to the gymnasium, library, and performing arts areas.

Located on a tight urban site, the building is situated to maximize north daylighting, while limiting solar exposure on the east and west façades. The site is organized with perimeter vehicular areas to allow uninterrupted student access to athletic and play areas. At the street level, the school will provide an engaging streetscape to reinforce its role in re-invigorating the urban neighborhood environment.

The school's architectural design expresses the social organization of the program and creates an appropriate climatic response to the environment. Aesthetically, the school expresses the forward-looking educational program while reflecting Dallas's tradition of regional modernism.

Sustainable features:

☼ Classrooms and labs situated to receive optimal northern daylight, which is ideal for study and minimizes cooling demand ☼ All of the classrooms placed on the north side of the building with limited solar exposure on east and west façades ☼ Program spaces in the southern portion of the building require minimal natural light and are situated with the ability to control the southern exposure ☼ Exterior landscaping is educational and resource efficient; water systems sustainably and efficiently accommodate harsh Texas sun, with drainage to meet the city's stringent stormwater protection plan ☼ A lush outdoor green space will give students an opportunity to learn about native plant life and history, with 10 Texas topographic "regions" included in the landscape design

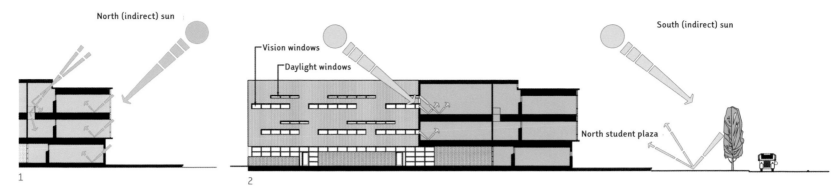

North (indirect) sun

South (indirect) sun

Vision windows

Daylight windows

North student plaza

1

2

3

4

1,2 Sustainability strategies

3 Auditorium

4 Lobby

5 Corridor

6 Library

Renderings: courtesy Perkins+Will

5

6

Hector Godinez High School – Santa Ana Unified School District

Santa Ana, California, USA
LPA, Inc.

Sustainable features:

✿ Natural, recycled and recyclable building materials ✿ Abundant trees, light-colored concrete, and extensive use of concrete pavers reduce the heat island effect, as does a parking structure for 80% of the parking ✿ Wetland and drainage basin for a portion of the site; roof drainage daylights into the basin to allow for water polishing and regeneration of ground water ✿ Landscape and domestic water usage is reduced by 30% ✿ Low precipitation irrigation heads and irrigation controllers using evapotranspiration rate sensors, rain gauges to automatically shut off the water, and automatic flow sensing to shut off and limit water waste in the event of a line break ✿ "Green screen" and landscape berming anchor the science labs to the earth and the adjacent wetlands ✿ Low-E insulated window glazing and a variety of shading features ✿ Energy usage and costs are reduced up to 13.3% more than required by the California Title 24 energy code in some buildings ✿ Thermal displacement ventilation system in the theater reduces energy for heating and cooling loads ✿ Automatic lighting controls for indirect and direct T8 fluorescent lighting in all classrooms and common areas

■ Hector Godinez High School is a direct result of a collaborative effort between four distinct public/government agencies: the Santa Ana Unified School District, the City of Santa Ana, the Discovery Heritage Museum & Nature Center, and the RSCCD Centennial Education Center. This 2500-student, 260,000-square-foot (24,000-square-meter) high school makes use of adjacent parkland for a total site size of 25 acres (10 hectares). Shared-use facilities include hard courts and playfields, as well as a gymnasium facility, and a 450-seat performing arts complex.

The high school relies heavily on its context to establish its imagery. The scale of the campus was dictated by the urban character of the main street, the environment of the nature center, and the activities in the industrial area to the west. The classroom wing and media/administration wing act as a buffer for sound and sight from the industrial area to the nature center and provide a reflecting wall for the nature center, performing as a sunscreen for the building.

Insulated skylights bring natural light into the classroom block hallways and typical classrooms harvest daylight with lighting controls. Good indoor air quality is promoted with the elimination of chalkboards and carpet. Concrete block is exposed in the classrooms, creating a visual interest and promoting thermal lag on the south and north exposures.

The single-story science labs are used as a scale mediator for the single-story nature center to the south and the two-story classroom block to the north. The building façades that face the wetland use berms and green screens to create a landscape canvas of indigenous plant material. This additional landscape minimizes the building's exposure from the wetland and promotes sustainable site design for stormwater runoff and the natural insulation of the buildings. The recycled metal roofing, composite siding material, and concrete block reinforce the special purpose of these buildings in the overall urban plan. The composite siding becomes an overhang and is designed to protect the openings so that the science labs are a working model of responsible sustainable design.

1

3

4

2

1 Aerial view of joint-use facility

2 The Zocalo and science village

3 Gymnasium

4 Science village

5

5 View along Main Street

6 View through classroom block

7 Performing arts interior

8 Performing arts exterior

9 Interior of science classroom

6

7

8

9

10

11

10 Administration

11 Performing arts lobby

12 Gymnasium

Photography: Costea Photography

12

High School for the Visual and Performing Arts

Los Angeles, California, USA
COOP HIMMELB(L)AU / HMC Architects

■ Located among downtown Los Angeles' burgeoning cultural landmarks and the arts district, the High School for the Visual and Performing Arts will be a flagship school for the Los Angeles Unified School District. The campus will complement the District's academic small learning communities (SLCs) with comprehensive facilities for dance, music, visual arts, and performing arts education.

In this urban context, the challenge was to create an open, educational space for 1500 students while maintaining security in this cultural downtown corridor. The result is a campus that embraces exterior circulation while establishing a protective perimeter. Each department building sits on the outer border of the site, overlooking various sections of Los Angeles to the exterior and a central courtyard to the interior. The flow between SLCs leads students through an expansive plaza level and recreational fields that create outdoor learning and gathering spaces. The design preserves the urban edge of the downtown LA community with a strong architectural statement, while creating a protected interior space dedicated to student education.

The High School for the Visual and Performing Arts has earned a Collaborative for High Performance Schools (CHPS) certification rating of 34, well above the average rating for this California-based, non-profit collaborative for sustainability. Though the campus program necessitates expansive energy-intensive indoor spaces, such as the 950-seat theater and adjacent lobby, the campus has exceeded energy performance criteria by 20 percent. Designers achieved such efficiency while maintaining connection elements with the community, including a two-story glass lobby and portal windows offering passersby a visual path into the life of the facility.

Sustainable features:

✿ Centrally located site: 50% of students live within the area or are near public transport ✿ Joint-use facilities include multipurpose/performance, library, gymnasium, athletic fields, and adjacent parks ✿ Multi-story classroom buildings minimize footprint to reduce site coverage ✿ Thermal comfort is enhanced through the use of operable windows, temperature, and lighting controls within each classroom ✿ High indoor air quality results from low-E interior materials including carpet, acoustical ceiling tiles, and rubber flooring ✿ Exceeds state electrical efficiency requirements by 20%

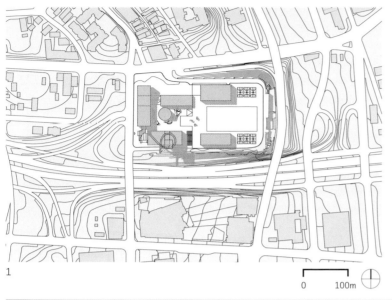

1

1 Site plan

2 Model view of public theater lobby and tower

3 View of the campus from Grand Avenue with lobby/theater and visual arts building

2

0   100m

3

4

5

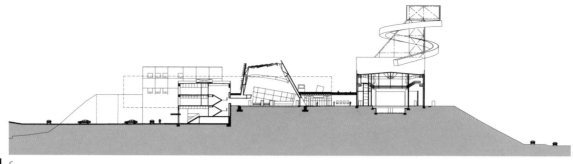

6

7

Holten-Richmond Middle School

Danvers, Massachusetts, USA
DiNisco Design Partnership

■ The new Holten-Richmond Middle School integrates two existing buildings, built in 1929 and 1931, that were originally the junior high school and high school. While it was a priority to maintain the historic character of the Holten and Richmond buildings by restoring the façades, the existing 95,000-square-foot (28,956-square-meter) interior space was totally reconfigured to meet modern educational requirements. Selective demolition was performed at the rear of the existing building to incorporate a contemporary addition that utilized design cues from the traditional original structure.

The school is on a restricted site, but an innovative solution to expand the site was found in collaboration between the School Department and the Town Department of Parks and Recreation. The students have full access to an adjoining park owned by the town during the day, and the school in turn is available for community use at night and on weekends. Public access to its modern core facilities, including the gymnasium, fitness center, performing arts center, assembly hall, and library has revitalized the neighborhood and transformed the school into the community center of Danvers.

The adjacency of the park also creates opportunities for families to use the facilities jointly during the school year, for spring/fall athletic events and throughout the summer for evening baseball games, town fairs, and special events. As an added benefit, sharing the existing fields between the school and the town reduced site development costs.

The durability and maintainability of the design and materials were carefully planned and are consistent with the town's philosophy of preserving its assets with quality materials and long-term maintenance.

Sustainable features:

✿ South-facing glass for direct solar heat gain, which is controlled by specifically designed sun shades for maximum heat in winter and maximum shade in summer ✿ Selected solar shades are fitted with photovoltaic cells to generate energy to reduce the electrical needs of the building ✿ Special light-sensing controls dim or turn off light fixtures when lighting needs are satisfied by daylighting ✿ Low-E glazing is specially formulated for each building elevation depending upon the solar exposure to increase optimum energy efficiency ✿ Lighting energy consumption is 0.93 watts per square foot ✿ Rainwater is collected and used for site irrigation ✿ 75% of materials exported from the site were sent to recycling plants; 5% of imported materials, primarily steel and concrete, were previously recycled ✿ Planted rock filters were added to improve upon code-mandated water quality measures ✿ The project received a Green Schools grant from the Massachusetts Technology Collaborative

1

3

1   Site plan

2   The historic Holten and Richmond buildings

3   The modern entrance unites the two historic buildings

2

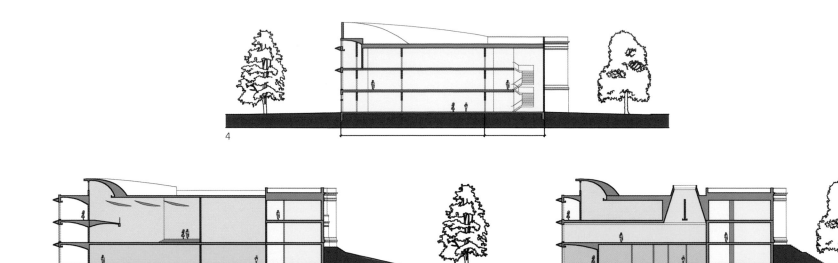

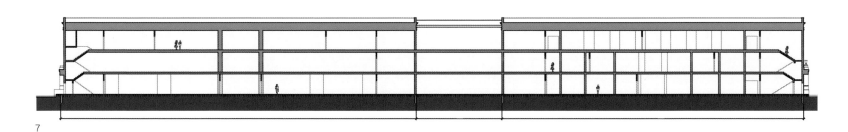

4   Building section at entry stair

5   Building section at auditorium/cafeteria

6   Building section at library

7   Longitudinal section

8   The contemporary addition at the rear of the school

9   Solar panels were incorporated into the contemporary addition

10 Exterior solar panels increase energy efficiency across the building

8

9

10

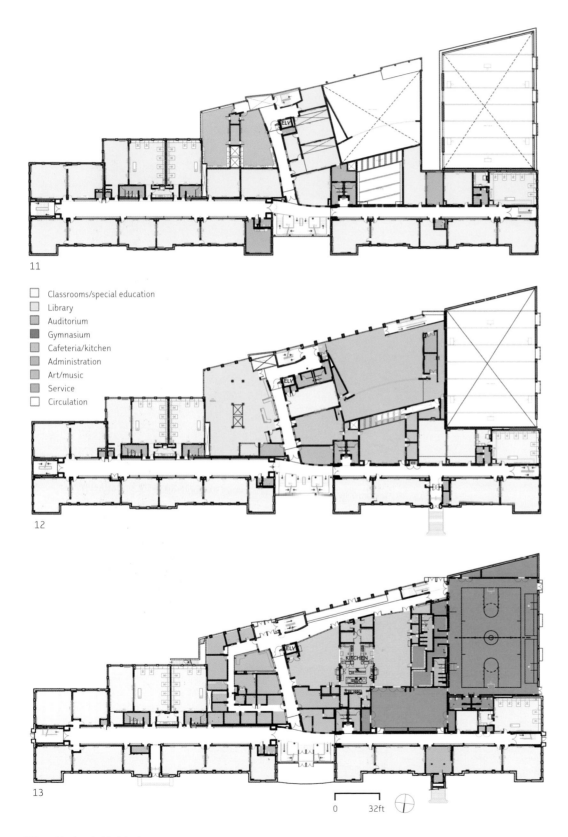

11

Classrooms/special education
Library
Auditorium
Gymnasium
Cafeteria/kitchen
Administration
Art/music
Service
Circulation

12

13

0   32ft

14

15

16

17

11 Third floor plan

12 Second floor plan

13 First floor plan

14 The front entrance floods the school with natural light

15 The cafeteria has flexible capacity

16 The gymnasium features natural daylighting

17 Band room

18 Second floor auditorium

Photography: Peter Vanderwarker

18

The International School, The Hague

The Hague, The Netherlands
Atelier PRO architekten

The International School The Hague (ISH) provides a learning and living environment for children from 0 to 18 years of age. It accommodates approximately 1400 children and 150 staff, representing more than 70 nationalities. It offers an international curriculum that is highly renowned and enjoys world-wide recognition.

The international curriculum provides continuous education, beginning with day care, kindergarten, the international primary curriculum, followed by the middle years' program and culminating in the International Baccalaureate. In addition the school provides other facilities for the international community in The Hague, including courses, exhibitions, cultural events, lectures, and meetings. The aim is to connect people through learning.

The building has a clear center, the "international plaza," which functions as the central entrance, the learning center, and as a meeting place. Each age group has its own "cluster" adjoining the central communal rooms, accessed via "lounges." The lounges are like living rooms for the different age groups. The construction concept is strongly oriented to the principle of independent learning, reflected in the many study rooms, laboratories, media center/library, and the layout of the clusters. Within and between the clusters, study and craft rooms are flexible, making it possible to respond to future educational developments without major structural alteration.

Sustainability was an important driver for the design of the building services installations. For educational purposes, displays are placed at the entrance, showing the power currently being generated by the building. All areas of the building are ventilated, cooled, and heated in a highly efficient way that is also decentralized, allowing different parts of the building to be used independently.

Sustainable features:

✿ The concrete floors of the building are used for cooling (concrete core cooling); during the night enough cooling is supplied to keep indoor temperatures at an acceptable level in summer, avoiding the need for an electrically driven cooling plant ✿ High-efficiency boilers combined with low-temperature heating system ✿ Adiabatic cooling of inlet air ✿ "Wind wall" for generating electrical power ✿ Photovoltaic cells generate electrical power ✿ Solar panels heat the tap water system ✿ Return air from the classrooms and offices is used to heat the atrium; air handling units are equipped with a heat recovery unit to heat up the fresh air by regaining heat from the exhaust air

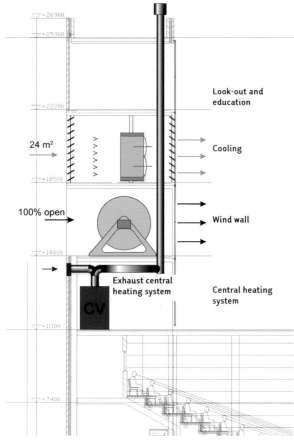

+26900
+25900

+22200

Look-out and
education

24 m²

Cooling

+18500

100% open

Wind wall

+14800

Exhaust central
heating system

CV

Central heating
system

+11100

+7400

1   Note: wind wall floor and cooling are interchangeable

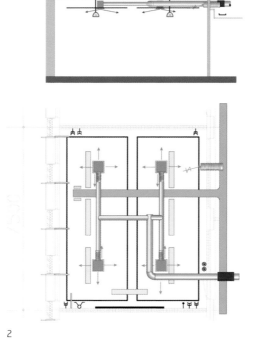

2

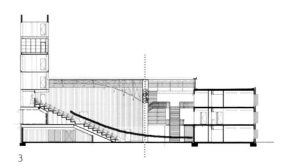

3

1 Section of installations tower

2 Concept diagram of classroom heating and
   cooling systems

3 Section of tower and auditorium

4 Section through plaza, facing south

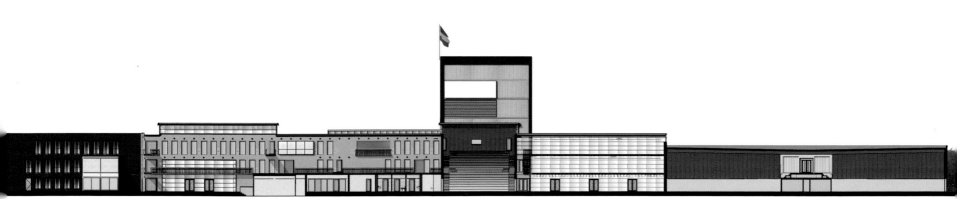

4

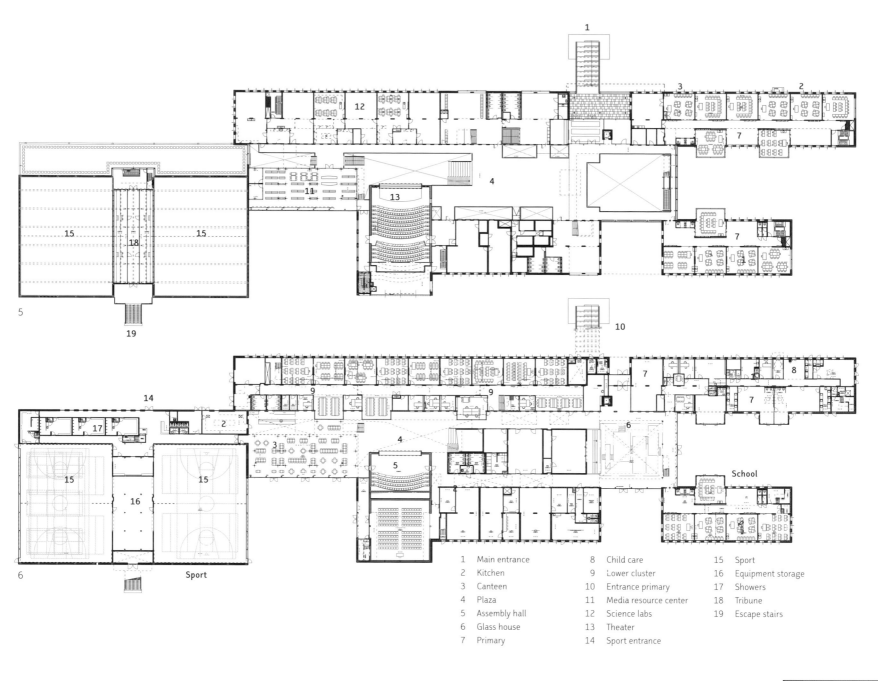

1	Main entrance	8	Child care	15	Sport
2	Kitchen	9	Lower cluster	16	Equipment storage
3	Canteen	10	Entrance primary	17	Showers
4	Plaza	11	Media resource center	18	Tribune
5	Assembly hall	12	Science labs	19	Escape stairs
6	Glass house	13	Theater		
7	Primary	14	Sport entrance		

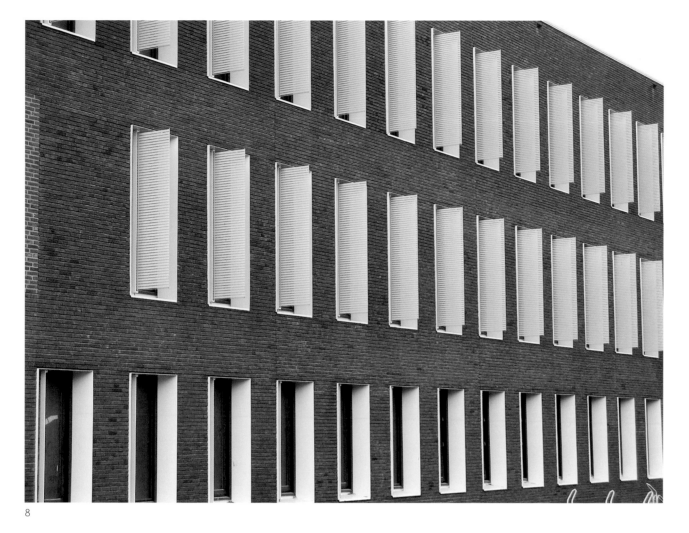

8

5 First floor plan

6 Ground floor plan

7 Section through plaza, facing north

8 Façade with movable glass sunscreens

Renderings: courtesy Atelier PRO

Lick-Wilmerding High School

San Francisco, California, USA
Pfau Architecture, Ltd.

■ The new technology and design center for the Lick-Wilmerding High School represents the school's unique dedication and appreciation for arts education. The design also provided the opportunity to create an environment that would encourage collaboration and inspire a sense of community for its users.

The school's integrated and demanding academic curriculum places a strong emphasis on the technical and fine arts—the only college preparatory school in the US with this program. Over the years, the school had nearly exhausted available opportunties to expand within its own property and felt forced to proceed with a building location on the eastern edge of the existing field. This move, dictated by the existing master plan, would drastically alter the experience of the school, cutting off the views of the distant hills.

Departing from the previous master plan, this design extends the lower level of the campus, placing the workshops at the heart, under the plane of the existing field. The workshops are now oriented toward each other, creating a shared work area that encourages interdisciplinary work and collaboration. The rest of the campus wraps around the centralized core, forming an understated design solution. The new student center/dining hall overlooks the workshops-level addition and connects through a stair to the lower level. The school's eastward views remain unimpeded; the distant hills remain an extension of the school's field and act as a borrowed landscape for the inhabitants of this small urban site. The roofs of the workshops are transformed into a series of terraced landscapes—a favorite spot for students to gather during lunch or between classes.

Sustainable features:

✿ Natural cross ventilation is used throughout for cooling ✿ Insulated and low-E glass is used throughout ✿ All buildings utilize earth as an insulation to limit temperature swings ✿ Louvered sun control elements are utilized at appropriate façades ✿ Sustainable harvested ipe wood is used ✿ Photovoltaic panels are integrated to lower energy cost and provide a useful educational tool ✿ Systems are integrated to plan for future photovoltaic panels on various roofs ✿ Windmills along I-280 are planned to provide power to the student lounge and become an important symbol to the community of Lick-Wilmerding's interest in educating the people who will help shape our sustainable future

1,2 Student cafeteria

3 View across field toward cafeteria

1

2

3

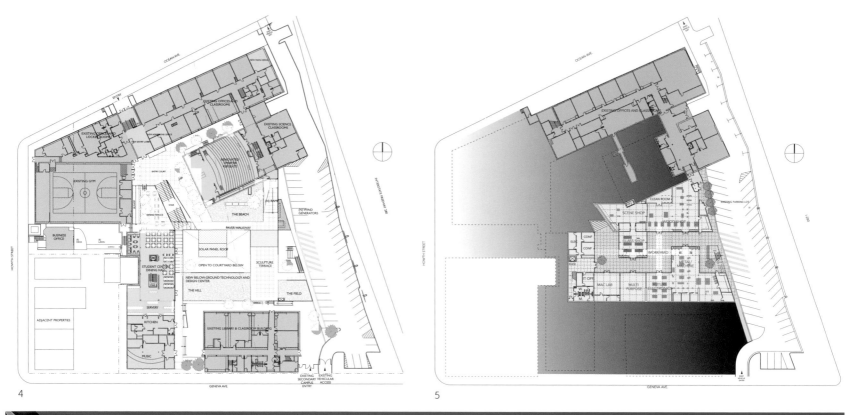

4

5

6

7

4   Field level floor plan

5   Lower level, technology and design center floor plan

6   View across field, toward cafeteria, with the articulated roofscapes of the shops

7   Student on bridge above the shops level

8   Student cafeteria

9   Exterior walkway, adjacent to student cafeteria

10 Center court

11 Looking down onto the shops level from the main school level

11

8

9

10

12

13

14

Photography: Tim Griffith

16

15

Mawson Lakes School

Mawson Lakes, South Australia, Australia
**Guida Moseley Brown Architects and
Russell & Yelland Architects**

■ Mawson Lakes School (Stage 1, 2004) is a public elementary school designed for 440 students in a new urban development in northern Adelaide.

The brief asked for a flexible innovative learning environment that supported "life-long learning" with a shift from single class groups to individual and team learning. Extensive consultation with students, staff, and community stakeholders further reinforced an emphasis on community and ecological sustainability, which is embodied in all aspects of the school, from the macro to the micro.

A series of "family units" are arranged along a covered circulation spine linking to multipurpose and administration buildings. Careful planning of relationships between internal spaces and safe semi-enclosed courtyards enhances flexibility of use, and provides ideal north–south orientation. Direct links between family units are provided by opening into these courtyards.

Challenging the notion of what a school should look like, the built form integrates planning to suit site constraints, curriculum innovations, passive solar design principles, active systems controlling thermal and air quality, and low-maintenance materials. Inside and outside spaces are given equal weight as stimulating, flexible places for learning .

Learning focus is brought to construction methods and materials by exposing a section of wall framing and insulation behind Perspex, clear power points, and showcasing different materials. Involvement in an art program to design the "face" of the school (a screen fence to the plaza), provided further opportunities for students to explore, understand, and control their immediate environment. As tour guides for the school's many visitors, the students demonstrate their understanding and valuing of issues of sustainability and the built environment.

Sustainable features:

✪ Efficient use of a small site by building hard up to the street edge on the east and opening out to shared school and community use open space on the north, west, and south ✪ Community links and efficiency through shared facilities use ✪ Cycle and walking paths provide safe access from the surrounding housing and community links ✪ Simple and repetitive building forms minimize construction waste ✪ Steel structural frame and plantation timber framing to enable easy future replanning, reuse, and recycling ✪ Low-maintenance, durable steel cladding ✪ Reduced energy consumption through orientation for breezes and solar control, appropriate distribution of openings, massive and lightweight materials, insulation, shading, and low-E glass ✪ Building Management Systems linked to thermal and solar chimneys to support thermal control ✪ Student use of web-based software with graphical display to adjust and monitor temperatures, power consumption, and the status of air conditioning and dampers ✪ North-facing windows to the courtyard and large south lights infuse the learning spaces with natural light ✪ Connection to the suburb's infrastructure of wetlands stormwater treatment and sewer/water recycling through gray water reticulation for irrigation ✪ An active recycling program for operational waste

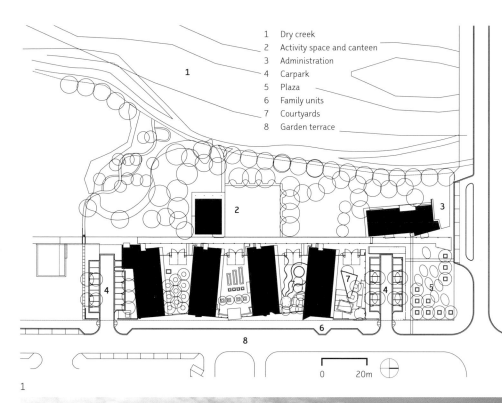

1 Dry creek
2 Activity space and canteen
3 Administration
4 Carpark
5 Plaza
6 Family units
7 Courtyards
8 Garden terrace

3

1 Site plan

2 Courtyards and circulation spine connect family units

3 Family units sit hard up to the street edge

1

2

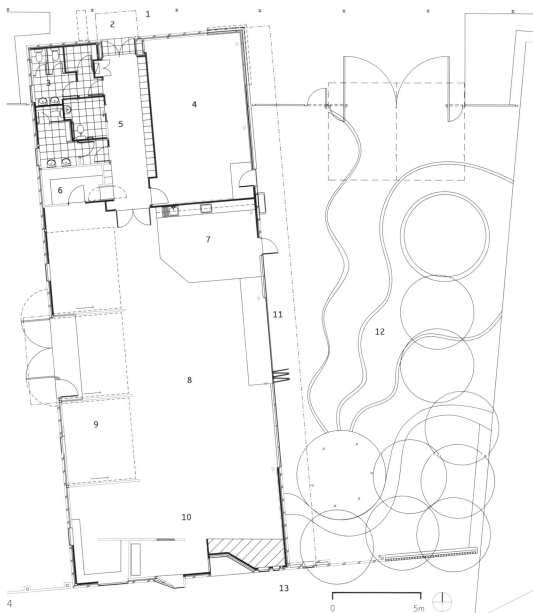

5

6

1 Walkway
2 Entry
3 Toilets
4 Specialist teaching (science/media)
5 Lockers
6 Store
7 Wet area (art)
8 Learning spaces
9 Movable panels
10 Small group spaces
11 Bi-fold doors
12 Secure courtyard
13 Garden terrace

0   5m

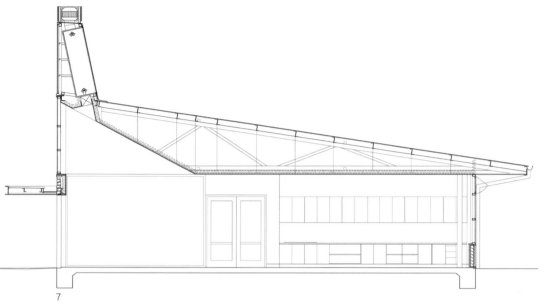

4 Typical family unit floor plan

5 Understanding of principles of energy efficiency achieved through active participation

6 Windows and semi-transparent screens connect buildings and courtyards with public street

7 Section

8 The covered spine connects the building with multipurpose and administration areas beyond

Photography: John Gollings (2,3,8); Steve Rendoulis (5,6)

7

8

Mead Middle School Gymnasium

Mead, Colorado, USA
Hutton Ford Architects

■ The design for the Mead Middle School's new gym incorporated a concept called "displacement ventilation." In a traditional ventilation system, heated or cooled air is forced from ceiling diffusers to the gym floor at high velocities that may be uncomfortable for students. This process is inefficient because warm air rises to the ceiling, creating stagnant air below. In contrast, displacement ventilation supplies fresh air at a low velocity from numerous outlets close to the floor. Air is displaced from the playing surface at a moderate rate and directed toward the ceiling, thus removing contaminants and odors. Displacement ventilation works with, instead of against, the basic physics of heated air rising. Supply air is directed over the floor surface and then rises as it is heated by internal sources, such as the students. Warm air high in the space is either exhausted or returned to the air handler for re-conditioning.

The gymnasium is daylighted by translucent windows on the south, and clear, insulated glass windows on the north. They are located high on the walls to reduce glare for students playing below and to wash the ceiling with daylight. Electric lights in the gymnasium are circuited in three zones: south, north, and center. The zones adjacent to windows are controlled by photocells that turn the lights on and off depending on the daylight levels. The center zone is controlled manually.

The combination of displacement ventilation, the high windows, and controlled electric lighting produced substantial cost savings in the school district's energy costs and addressed other concerns with the district's older gyms such as inadequate lighting, poor acoustics, and poor air quality.

Sustainable features:

✿ Displacement ventilation reduces noise, improves air quality, and saves energy ✿ Initial construction cost of HVAC system was similar to traditional system ✿ Downsized roof top mechanical unit as a result of the displacement ventilation approach ✿ Bleachers on wall are used as an air diffuser ✿ South-facing translucent clerestory provides abundant daylight without direct beam penetration ✿ North-facing clear glass clerestory balances daylight inside space ✿ Fluorescent lighting provides quick on/off capability ✿ Photocell controls monitor available daylight and turn off unnecessary lights ✿ Light-colored interior surfaces enhance daylight reflection and distribution ✿ Long life, low-maintenance exterior walls utilize local brick and concrete block

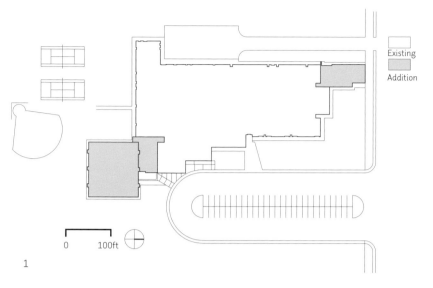

1   Site plan

2   Detail view of gymnasium entry

3   View from southeast

4   Daylighting/electric lighting diagram

5   Displacement ventilation diagram

6   Detail view of daylighting at north wall and displacement ventilation grilles in the retracted bleachers

7   Detail view of displacement ventilation chase and translucent windows at the south wall

8   Gymnasium with electric lights on

9   Gymnasium with lights off, showing daylighting

Photography: Ed LaCasse (2,3,6-8); Kari-elin Mock (9)

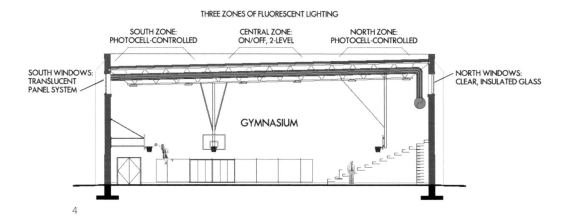

THREE ZONES OF FLUORESCENT LIGHTING

SOUTH ZONE:
PHOTOCELL-CONTROLLED

CENTRAL ZONE:
ON/OFF, 2-LEVEL

NORTH ZONE:
PHOTOCELL-CONTROLLED

SOUTH WINDOWS:
TRANSLUCENT
PANEL SYSTEM

NORTH WINDOWS:
CLEAR, INSULATED GLASS

GYMNASIUM

4

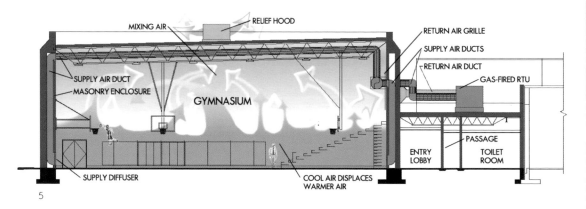

MIXING AIR   RELIEF HOOD

RETURN AIR GRILLE

SUPPLY AIR DUCTS

RETURN AIR DUCT

GAS-FIRED RTU

SUPPLY AIR DUCT

MASONRY ENCLOSURE

GYMNASIUM

SUPPLY DIFFUSER

COOL AIR DISPLACES
WARMER AIR

ENTRY
LOBBY

PASSAGE

TOILET
ROOM

5

6

7

8

9

Newark Science Park High School

Newark, New Jersey, USA
Einhorn Yaffee Prescott Architecture
& Engineering, P.C.

■ This new science magnet high school is a dynamic model of how technology can be utilized in educational delivery. It's one of the first beneficiaries of a capital program spearheaded by a state construction program to build innovative new schools. The mission of Newark Science Park High School is to transform the teaching and learning of mathematics and science.

The high school is organized around an "Academic Village" that supports the convergence of natural sciences, mathematics, and technology with the social/behavioral sciences and the humanities into a coherent whole. The new school uses these groundbreaking educational ideas to help foster social progress and the renaissance of this economically depressed area. The high school provides educational and recreational facilities to the local community, and develops ethical leaders who, from the environment in which they learned, have the passion of innovation instilled in them.

Critical to building these skills of learning is the link between teaching science and using the school itself and the grounds as a hands-on laboratory to learn about sustainable design. Geothermal boreholes are located over the playing fields and parking lots. Energy recovery units recapture exhaust air temperature to provide high-energy savings and comfort. Variable frequency drives and high-efficiency motors are located throughout the various systems. Besides being able to observe first-hand how these systems operate, building controls for all of these are accessible to students for analysis through "read only" computer stations. From the development of this unity of knowledge, it is possible for students to learn from different fields of study and to apply their experiences to the full range of human perspectives.

Sustainable features:

✿ The structure is expressed within the building, which serves as an educational tool in addition to material supplies and costs saved during construction ✿ Photovoltaic panels are used to power student experiments within the building ✿ 16-foot (5-meter) floor-to-floor heights allow daylighting controls using sunscreens, light shelves, indirect lighting with light sensor controls, and introducing natural daylighting at many opportunities such as the atrium, stairwells, and gymnasium ✿ The geothermal heat pump system cuts energy consumption by approximately 30%; room-by-room, zone-by-zone heating and cooling increase user comfort and allow heating energy to be moved from warm zones to cool zones ✿ The project includes a geothermal well field consisting of 375 holes ✿ The main atrium ("Village Commons") utilizes acoustical control, increased ventilation, and CO_2 monitoring ✿ The school incorporates healthy and high-performance features, designed for LEED Silver certification, made possible by the aggressive pursuit of rebates totaling more than $1 million

1 The new science magnet school, in a dense urban area, is the culmination of ambitious planning by the school district, local community groups, and public and private institutions

2 Conceptually, the building maximizes the use of the tight site—the articulation of the building massing, the use of brick, metal panels, and glass, and the expression of photovoltaic panels celebrate science and the learning opportunities within

3 The school is organized as four learning modules centered around an atrium, encouraging interdisciplinary team teaching

2

3

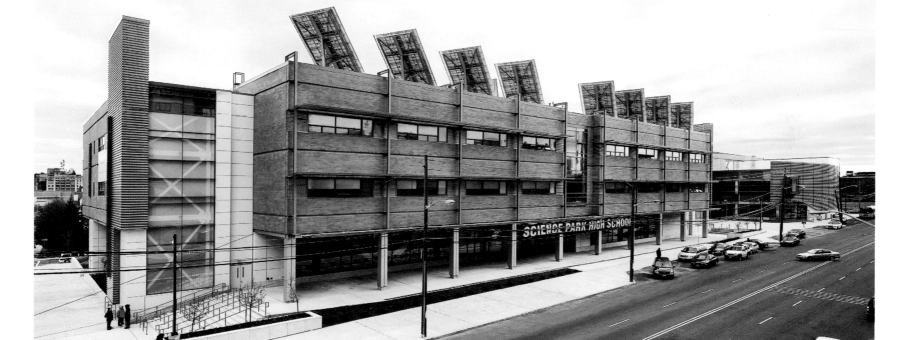

1

4

4   The information network is linked to universities, supported by their staff; the school is
    the first to be connected to the state's higher education network

5   Natural daylighting in all public spaces was a priority from the early design phases of
    the project

Photography: Chun Y Lai Photography

5

Phelps Academy Center, Phillips Exeter Academy

Exeter, New Hampshire, USA
William H. Grover, FAIA and
Sheri Bryant Dieso, AIA, LEED of
Centerbrook Architects and Planners

■ Phillips Exeter Academy asked Centerbrook to renovate an historic 1930 science classroom building into a new Student Center. The school also wanted the new building to incorporate the principals of sustainable design and to serve as a teaching tool that would influence the attitudes and behavior of those who use it.

The science building was originally built as part of an academic quadrangle of brick buildings at the center of the campus. While it opened to the quadrangle, it had no entrance on its other major façade facing Tan Lane, one of the school's main campus streets. This was a serious impairment to campus circulation.

The new Phelps Academy Center now provides a home for student activities and clubs at the heart of the Exeter campus. At its center is a new oval atrium, the "Agora," an informal gathering place that also acts as a campus artery through the building, connecting the quadrangle to Tan Lane. The Student Center has become a campus hub, highly regarded and well used by students, faculty, and staff.

The Center includes the campus "Grill," the post office, day student lounge, arts and crafts rooms, club rooms, music practice rooms, game rooms, the student-run radio station, lounges, meeting rooms, and auditorium.

The Academy Center has been designed so that many of its sustainable characteristics are evident to those who use the building. Plaques describing the materials and systems used in the building are prominently displayed. The Center has received a LEED Silver rating from the U. S. Green Building Council.

Sustainable features:

✦Erosion control to reduce negative impacts on water and air quality ✦Building reuse with minimal additional footprint ✦Zero increase in stormwater run-off ✦Shaded impervious surfaces; light-colored flat roofs and walking surfaces for greater reflectance ✦Captured stormwater directed to reclaimed cistern for irrigation; no potable water used ✦Infrared sensor flushing mechanisms ✦Water consumption reduced by 30% ✦Zero use of CFC-based refrigerants ✦Reduced energy consumption (compared to energy cost budget) by 30% ✦Reuse of existing chiller from adjacent building to cool new building ✦Lighting control system ✦Continuous metering of building equipment for lighting and HVAC systems ✦Recycling stations throughout building ✦96.7% of construction, demolition, and land clearing waste recycled ✦Recycled materials used in building ✦Local and regional materials and products ✦Ventilation complies with ASHRAE 62 ✦CO_2 monitoring system ✦Air quality management plan, during construction and pre-occupancy ✦Low- or no-VOC emitting materials for sealants, adhesives, carpets, and paints ✦Entryway systems to capture dirt and particulates ✦Used existing oak tree (forced to remove) for wood trim, conference table, and plaques identifying sustainable choices throughout building ✦"Building as Educator" sustainable displays and identifier plaques throughout the building ✦The LEED system was used and monitored throughout the design and construction phases

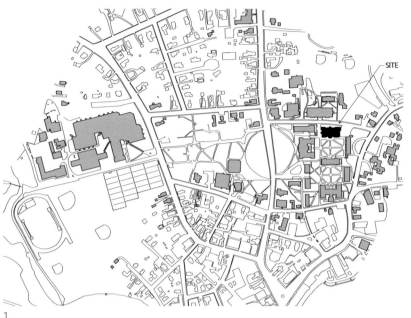

1 Campus plan

2 The Agora, a gathering place and campus artery; Tan Lane entrance at left, quadrangle entrance at right. Note built-in recycling containers at right.

3 The quadrangle

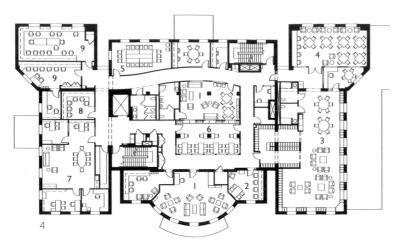

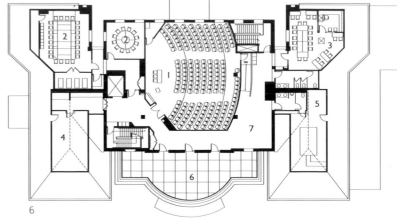

1 Student club room   6 Club resource room
2 Student council   7 Student activities office
3 Day student lounge   8 Literary club room
4 Day student quiet study   9 School newspaper
5 Meeting room

1 Forum   5 Mechanical
2 Meeting room   6 Outdoor terrace
3 Study skills/group tutoring   7 Lobby
4 Storage

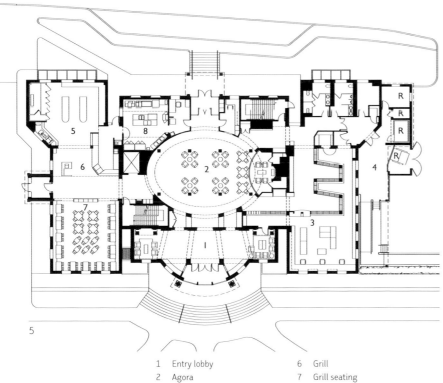

1 Entry lobby   6 Grill
2 Agora   7 Grill seating
3 Post office   8 Kitchen
4 Loading dock   9 Recycling
5 Convenience store

Photography: Jeff Goldberg/Esto

8

9

Primary School

Gando, Boulgou, Burkina Faso
Diébédo Francis Kéré

Burkina Faso is among the poorest countries in the world. With an illiteracy rate of more than 80 percent, the majority of its people have no alternatives to agriculture as a living.

Architect Diébédo Francis Kéré was born in the village of Gando, and was the first person from his village to study abroad. He reinvested his knowledge as an architect into the urgently needed construction of a new school in Gando.

Guided by principles of sustainable development, Mr. Kéré stressed the importance of the use of clay as one of the main building materials. Although cheap and readily available, when used in traditional building methods it performed poorly compared to more expensive, imported materials. Local people were taught how to refine clay and local materials, and how different construction techniques could further improve the performance.

The building is designed to be aesthetically uplifting, while optimizing protection against the harsh climatic conditions. The building is aligned from east to west and the floor plan consists of three rectangular volumes. The classrooms are arranged linearly, separated by covered areas for recreation and outdoor lessons.

The densely packed clay blocks of the walls and ceiling help moderate the room temperature. Elegantly simple slats at the windows combine shade and ventilation. A ring beam both links the classrooms and provides the structural base for the roof of corrugated metal sheeting. Steel supports lift the roof structure above the ceiling, creating spaces through which cooling air flows freely. The walls are shaded from sun and torrential rain by the overhanging roof.

Opened in 2001, the school has more than 350 pupils. The construction of teachers' accommodation, with standards to match the school building, followed. The school not only provides education for the village children, but is used to pass on new skills and knowledge to the entire community. Growing numbers of students meant that an extension became necessary. The new complex was completed at the end of 2006.

This project was the recipient of an Aga Khan Award for Architecture in 2004.

Sustainable features:

✿ Local materials are used ✿ The initially untrained village inhabitants provided local labor, under instruction by the architect; now, Gando villagers are being hired to work on other public projects due to their new construction skills ✿ The construction evoked a strong cooperation among the villagers involved; it has become the central point of the village ✿ Intelligent construction provides air flow without any artificial ventilation, resulting in comfortable indoor conditions ✿ A comparably low-budget construction ✿ Multiplier effect: neighboring villages follow the same model of community mobilization to build schools for themselves

1 Elevations

2 Relationship of roof, façade, and foundations

3 Overall view

2

3

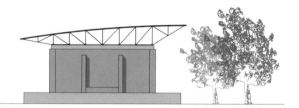

West elevation

East elevation

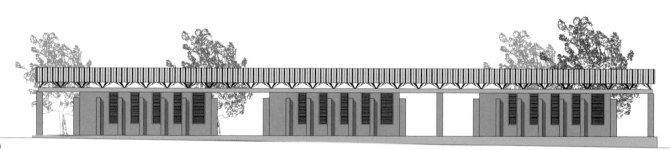

North elevation

South elevation

1

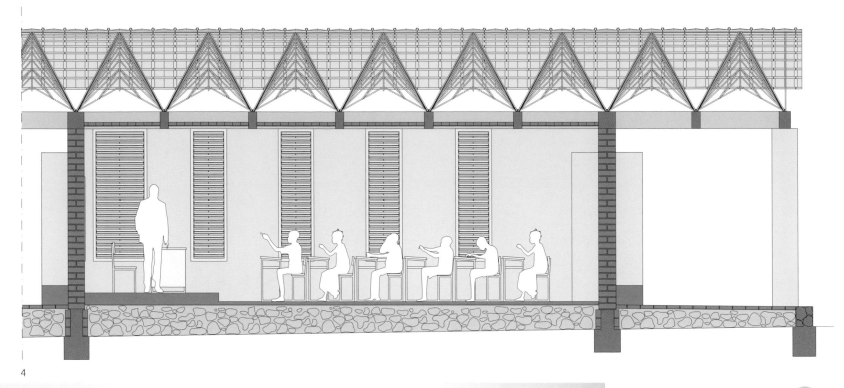

4

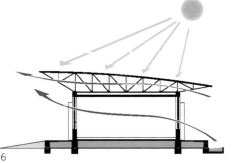

6

5

7

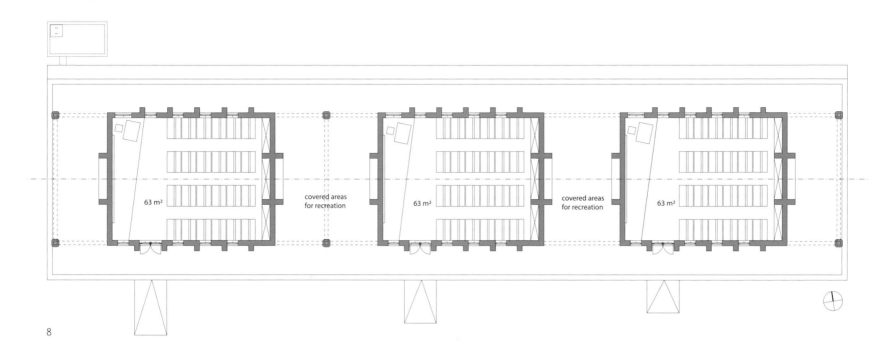

63 m²

covered areas for recreation

63 m²

covered areas for recreation

63 m²

8

4   Longitudinal section

5   Detail of building corner

6   Climatic scheme

7   Roof detail

8   Floor plan

9   Classroom interior

Photography: Simeon Duchoud/
Aga Khan Award for Architecture

9

Rosa Parks School

Portland, Oregon, USA
Dull Olson Weekes Architects

■ Rosa Parks School is designed, in part, to teach the building's users how to be good stewards of the environment. Students will discover how carefully preserved trees shade the site, prevent erosion, and store water. They'll learn how the vibrant vegetated bioswales that dot the property absorb, treat, and then channel all of the stormwater from the school into deep underground wells. Over time, they will discover that the native and drought-tolerant plants used require 50 percent less irrigation than more traditional choices.

Inside, the building demonstrates a range of cost-effective green measures. According to energy models, the campus will be 29 percent more efficient than required by the Oregon Energy Code. One of the most evident features is the extensive incorporation of natural daylight, which brightens the rooms, reduces lighting-related electricity consumption, and improves learning.

At Rosa Parks, the air is cleaner than in most buildings for several reasons. Builders kept construction debris out of heating and cooling ducts, mitigated the potential of mold developing in building materials stored onsite, and kept a clean "house" during construction to control dust and other pollutants. The team also used low-toxic and non-toxic building materials and sophisticated air filters, and carefully flushed the indoor air before the school opened to cleanse it of any lingering pollutants. The classroom wing is equipped with a displacement ventilation system that results in air quality that is superior to that of traditional mixing ventilation systems.

The students at Rosa Parks have learned to practice the "3 Rs": reduce, reuse, and recycle. So it shouldn't surprise them that contractors diverted more than 90 percent of construction waste by volume from the landfill by carefully sorting and then recycling the material. As much as 10 percent of the materials used in the building contain recycled content. A green "trash train" that services the entire neighborhood picks up recyclable materials and garbage from the school.

Sustainable features:

✿ Sensors automatically adjust building lighting in response to daylight levels ✿ Energy-efficient windows and skylights with a low-E coating reduce heat gain and loss ✿ Exterior sun shades and interior light shelves on east- and south-facing windows disperse daylight throughout the rooms, and reduce glare and overheating ✿ Operable windows bring in fresh outside air and cool the rooms naturally ✿ Limited parking spaces and incentives for carpooling ✿ Demonstration 1.1 kW solar panel installation with interactive display and supporting classroom curriculum ✿ Highly reflective roof to reduce heat island effect ✿ Onsite stormwater retention and treatment ✿ Access to school is 90% bicycle or pedestrian ✿ Monitoring of air quality to ensure optimum performance ✿ Use of regional materials ✿ Low-flow toilets and sinks

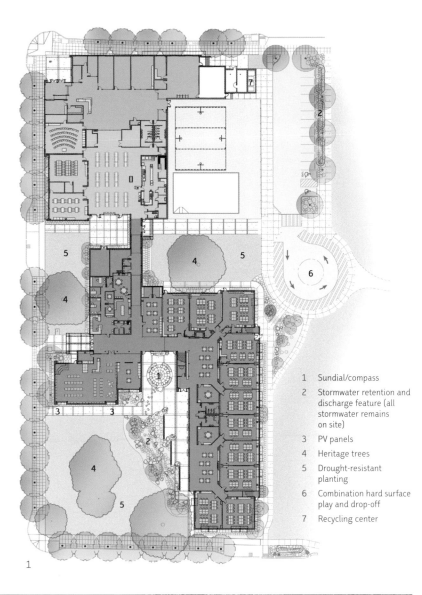

1 Site plan

2 Building was organized to protect existing trees

3 Large overhangs and vertical sunscreen on east side

1 Sundial/compass

2 Stormwater retention and discharge feature (all stormwater remains on site)

3 PV panels

4 Heritage trees

5 Drought-resistant planting

6 Combination hard surface play and drop-off

7 Recycling center

1

2

3

4

5

6

7

4   PV panels

5   Human sundial and compass

6   Vertical sunscreens protect east face
     of building

7   Stormwater detention and outdoor
     educational feature

8

9

8   Daylight penetration

9   Extended learning area

10 Light shelf and transparency allow daylight penetration

Photography: Gary Wilson Photo/Graphic

10

Sidwell Friends Middle School

Washington, DC, USA
KieranTimberlake Associates LLP

■ The Sidwell Friends School sought to give voice to an aesthetic derived from the Quaker ethic of environmental stewardship. The building acts as the central teacher in an environmental curriculum through which students witness natural and human-created systems at work. The entire campus is served by a central energy plant housed in the building, allowing greater control of energy resources and providing a demonstration of responsible energy use to students. The building employs mechanically assisted natural ventilation to minimize the need for artificial cooling. Classrooms are oriented to optimize natural lighting as the primary daytime illumination source. Photovoltaic panels and solar thermal technologies further reduce energy consumption.

The reclaimed wood cladding of the addition extends onto the existing building as sunshades, revealing orientation. North windows are unscreened, screens at south windows are horizontal, and screens at the east and west windows are vertical. Wood on the west elevation is arrayed vertically and angled for minimal solar penetration and maximum penetration of daylight. Behind the wood solar shading is a wood rain screen wall designed to shed most water but to remain open to the movement of air. The wood cladding was fabricated off-site in large sections to minimize site impact and the embodied energy of on-site fabrication.

Working in collaboration with Andropogon Associates, the landscape was transformed into a constructed wetland that treats and recycles building waste water on site for gray water use in the building, providing students with a vivid example of how such systems work in nature. Green roof vegetation holds and filters rainwater; gutters and downspouts direct rainwater to a biology pond, which supports native habitat. The developed landscape now serves as a unifying quadrangle in which existing and new buildings contribute to a purposeful and articulate whole.

Sustainable features:

✿ A constructed wetland treats building wastewater on site and recycles it for gray water use in the building ✿ Green roof vegetation holds and filters rainwater; gutters and downspouts direct rainwater to a biology pond, which will support native habitat ✿ Building orientation, passive and mechanically assisted ventilation, and solar chimneys reduce the need for supplemental energy for heating and cooling ✿ Window placement, skylights, and light shelves maximize use of natural light in new and existing classrooms ✿ 5% of the building's total electrical load is generated by photovoltaic panels ✿ Recycled, rapidly renewable and locally produced materials such as gypsum, linoleum, bamboo and agrofiber board are used as finishes in the building ✿ Reclaimed greenheart timber is used for interior wood flooring and exterior decking; copings, site walls, and walkways are of reclaimed stone ✿ Exterior wood cladding and sunscreens are made of reclaimed western red cedar; vertical sunscreens are oriented to balance thermal performance with daylighting ✿ Paints, carpets, and adhesives are selected for low emission of volatile organic compounds ✿ Energy performance is optimized with energy-efficient lighting with daylighting and occupancy controls, HVAC economizer, demand-controlled ventilation, variable speed fans and pumps, energy recovery, and high efficiency boilers and chillers

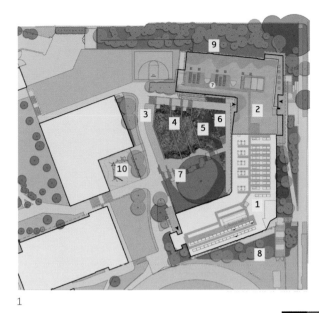

1   Existing middle school
2   Middle school addition with green roof
3   Trickle filter with interpretive display
4   Wetlands for wastewater treatment
5   Rain garden
6   Pond
7   Outdoor classroom
8   Butterfly meadow
9   Woodland screen at neighborhood edge
10   Play equipment

1

1   Site plan

2   Exterior view of addition through constructed wetland

2

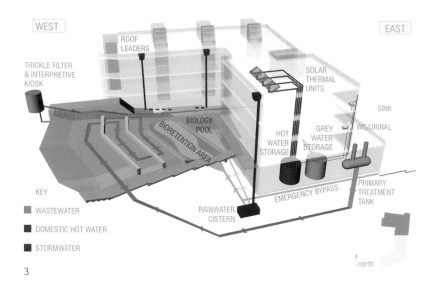

3 Wastewater, stormwater and domestic hot water management schematic

4 View of planted roof, garden, and solar chimneys

5 Detail of west entrance at courtyard

6 Reclaimed wood cladding was fabricated off-site in large sections

7

8

9

7   Abundant use of daylighting in library; artificial illumination is controlled by sensors

8   Reclaimed and rapidly renewable materials are used for building finishes

9   Wood solar shading arrayed vertically, as seen from interior

Photography: Barry Halkin

Drawings: Andropogon Associates; KieranTimberlake Associates

Solana Pacific Elementary School

San Diego, California, USA
HMC Architects

■ Located in a unique coastal region of San Diego, Solana Pacific Elementary School was conceived with energy and sustainable sensitivity from the earliest phase. This 78,000-square-foot (7246-square-meter) facility's orientation responds to wind and solar access, taking advantage of the prevailing breezes for natural cooling, solar gain for heating, and proper protection through shading.

The two-story design created a smaller envelope, reducing energy loss through its exterior, while clustering and positioning of the classrooms provided opportunities to reduce materials and energy resources. High-performance glazing systems, combined with operable clerestory windows, allow daylight to enhance the learning environment, while reducing and controlling heat gain and glare.

The facility's design maximized the use of recycled materials, providing a palette that respects resources and environmental quality. Careful selection of mechanical and electrical building systems provided efficiency. Effective solutions include a central digital control and monitoring system, electronic ballast lighting, occupancy sensors, T-8 lamps, and dimming systems. Roof extensions and a "white roof" were also used to control levels of heat gain.

Surpassing California's rigorous Title 24 standards for energy efficiency by 27 percent, the project saves the school district approximately 315,000 kWh of electricity and 830 therms of natural gas, or $51,600 at current energy rates, each year.

Solana Pacific Elementary School achieved a Collaborative for High Performance Schools (CHPS) certification rating of 34 points, well above the average rating for this California-based, non-profit collaborative for sustainability. The school was also awarded the 2005 Savings by Design Energy Efficiency Integration Citation for Design Excellence from Savings by Design and the AIA California Council, and the 2005 Council of Educational Facility Planners, International (CEFPI) Project of Distinction Award.

Sustainable features:

✿ Building orientation and environmental response ✿ Small building envelope ✿ Operable clerestory windows ✿ High-performance dual-pane glazing ✿ No- or low-VOC building materials ✿ High-efficiency lighting system ✿ Efficient mechanical design ✿ Drought-tolerant native plants ✿ Cool "white" roof ✿ Low-flow toilets and water-saving fixtures ✿ Covered walkways/shading structures

1 The two-story solution created a smaller exterior building envelope, thereby reducing energy losses

1

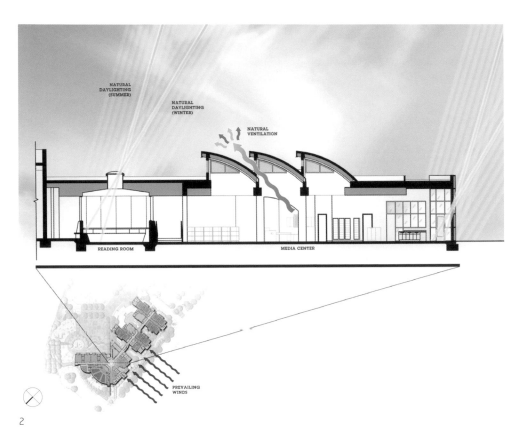

NATURAL
DAYLIGHTING
(SUMMER)

NATURAL
DAYLIGHTING
(WINTER)

NATURAL
VENTILATION

READING ROOM

MEDIA CENTER

PREVAILING
WINDS

2

3

2 Ideal orientation maximizes opportunities and minimizes undesirable energy impacts

3 High-performance glazing on classroom windows helps reduce heat and allows for daylighting

4 Protected entry limits solar gain, but allows for ample natural light

Photography: John Durant Photography (1); Hewitt Garrison Photography (3,4)

4

St Leonard's College, Sustainability Centre

Bangholme, Victoria, Australia
FMSA Architects

Sustainable features:

✺ North orientation to best respond to the microclimate and maximize northern sunlight ✺ Solar chimneys provide heated air in winter and induce cross-ventilation in summer ✺ Reversible ceiling fans redistribute rising heat in winter and enhance cooling effects in summer ✺ Retractable awnings and verandas provide shade from excessive heat ✺ Passive cooling through louvered ventilation evaporative panels coupled to rainwater storage tanks ✺ Further cross-ventilation is encouraged by large sliding doors to both north and south façades and operable skylights ✺ Thermal mass is incorporated through the use of concrete floors; solar hot water panels with LP gas-boosted hydronic system provide further heating ✺ Use of materials including lightweight high-insulation wall cladding, natural timber plywood internal linings, and compress straw ceiling panels ✺ Drought-resistant native vegetation minimizes water use ✺ Intelligent metering systems to monitor building's efficiency ✺ Photovoltaic panels and wind turbine generate electricity ✺ Twin rainwater storage tanks

■ The Sustainability Centre at St Leonard's College has been designed in response to a curriculum that looks forward to offering an education for a sustainable future.

The model of sustainability looks to the 1992 Earth Summit in Rio De Janiero, which provided a base for students' learning on a hierarchy of four overlays:

· The first overlay, centered on the notion of personal sustainability, seeks individual understanding in health and education, and balance in the demands of life.

· The second overlay relates to socio-cultural sustainability and looks to understand the history, geography, social studies, politics, and economics of our societies.

· The third concentrates on the sustainable understanding of the environmental overlay, which encompasses the challenges of global warming, loss of bio-diversity, dwindling reserves, and comprehension of the impacts and ways of how to reduce our environmental footprint.

· The fourth overlay focuses on urban sustainability, which considers our infrastructure and how we organise the way we live—systems of education, transport, health, and essential services.

FMSA views the design process as a response to the client's philosophy, the business plan, or school curriculum of the institution. Understanding the ambitions of a curriculum, the pedagogy, and the ways in which learning can be embraced is central to developing a design that responds to these issues.

The Sustainability Centre aims to touch all these overlays of understanding and exploration of our sustainable future. Not only is the building a working example of minimizing and conserving resources, it also acts as a working model in which students can participate in managing their environment.

Such an exemplary building can then engage with the development of student ideas for their own projects. The flexible space within allows student project groups to work, display, and store their results, promoting the exchange and continual evolution of ideas.

This exciting center is a new learning environment that not only engages and interacts with students, but also inspires creative responses and imaginative outcomes.

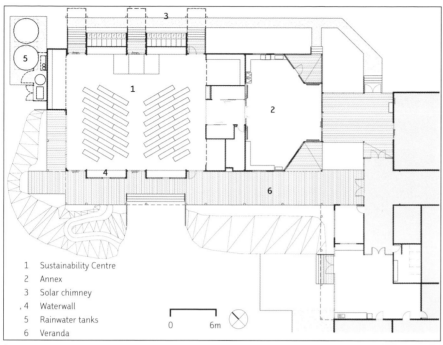

1 Sustainability Centre
2 Annex
3 Solar chimney
4 Waterwall
5 Rainwater tanks
6 Veranda

0   6m

1

1 Floor plan

2 Rear façade with drought-
   resistant landscaping around
   perimeter veranda decking

3 Front façade

3

4 Conceptual diagram of passive heating during winter

5 Conceptual diagram of passive cooling during summer

6 Façade detail with photovoltaic panels and solar chimney ventilation cowls

7 Façade detail of solar chimney and retractable awnings

8 Interior view

Photography: Mark Munro

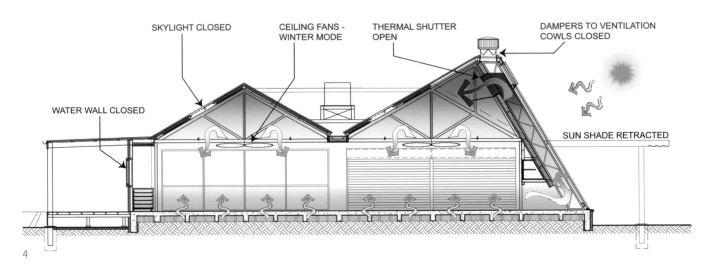

SKYLIGHT CLOSED

CEILING FANS - WINTER MODE

THERMAL SHUTTER OPEN

DAMPERS TO VENTILATION COWLS CLOSED

WATER WALL CLOSED

SUN SHADE RETRACTED

4

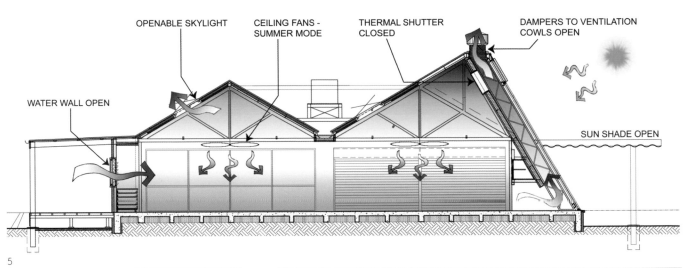

OPENABLE SKYLIGHT

CEILING FANS - SUMMER MODE

THERMAL SHUTTER CLOSED

DAMPERS TO VENTILATION COWLS OPEN

WATER WALL OPEN

SUN SHADE OPEN

5

6

7

The Dalles Middle School

The Dalles, Oregon, USA
BOORA Architects

The Dalles Middle School replaces a crumbling, outdated middle school on the same site, located near the core of downtown The Dalles. The new 96,765-square-foot (8990-square-meter) facility exemplifies energy conservation achieved through high-performance design.

An integrated design approach that involves all systems, materials, and program areas, as well as architectural and engineering disciplines, has significantly increased building efficiency. The building is oriented on an east–west axis, allowing the north- and south-facing classrooms to avoid east and west sun during the hottest periods of the day. High-performance glazing on 90 percent of all occupied rooms minimizes glare and heat gain, while exterior light shelves and vertical sunscreen louvers on the east and west façades diffuse sunlight without blocking views and bounce light deeper into classrooms. Skylights, clerestories, and Solatubes® provide daylight to typically darker interior spaces such as circulation routes, the gymnasium, the cafeteria, and classrooms. In addition, the school is naturally ventilated by wind turbines when outside weather is moderate (55–75 °F/13–24 °C), while a conventional fan system provides mechanical ventilation when outside temperatures are too low or too high, or if carbon dioxide sensors demand increased air movement. Using geothermal principles, a water source heat pump extracts heat from ground water captured from nearby dewatering wells. The existing infrastructure was designed and built to remove water from the adjacent hillside and thereby stabilize a landslide. Drawing water for the heat pump from these wells eliminated the need to drill holes for the system and saved the school district $500,000. After this water has been used in the building, it irrigates the school's playfields, saving the school district an additional $17,000 per year in water costs.

Daylighting, natural wind-driven ventilation, and a water source heat pump have reduced the annual energy consumption of the building by 45–50 percent below code, and will help the school achieve LEED Gold certification, which is currently pending.

Sustainable features:

✺ Wind-driven ventilation ✺ Water source heat pump using geothermal principles extracts heat from ground water to warm the building and reverses the process to cool it ✺ High-performance window glazing on 90% of all occupied rooms ✺ Exterior light shelves bounce light deeper into classrooms ✺ Vertical sunscreen louvers on the east and west façades diffuse sunlight without blocking views ✺ Skylights, clerestories, and Solatubes at interior classrooms, circulation routes, and common spaces allow all spaces to share daylight ✺ Wind turbine vents for ventilation with a back-up conventional fan system ✺ Auxiliary mechanical ventilation system turns on automatically if outside temperatures are too low or too high, or if carbon dioxide sensors required greater ventilation ✺ Energy-efficient fluorescent T-5 lights ✺ Individual occupancy and daylighting sensors in classrooms ✺ Drought-resistant landscaping ✺ 176 bicycle spots and charging station for future electric cars ✺ Woods, paints, and sealers that meet strict guidelines for reduced off-gassing ✺ Stained concrete exterior walls are durable and low maintenance, while providing thermal lag at the south-facing walls, much like adobe structures from the American southwest

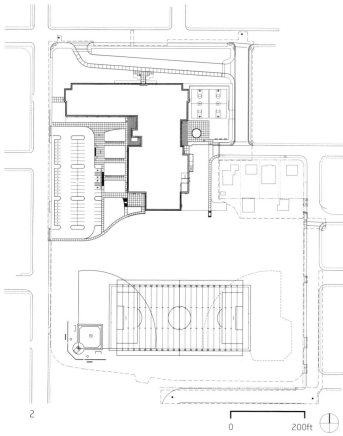

1

1 The entry courtyard bridges the classroom wing that is oriented east-west for optimal solar control with the commons and arts and athletic spaces that are oriented north-south for optimal thermal control

2 Site plan

3 In the commons and athletic spaces, concrete slabs and concrete masonry walls are used as thermal masses to stabilize internal air temperatures throughout the year

2

0   200ft

3

4 A diagram from the design process shows how ground water from nearby dewatering wells is directed to the school's water source heat pump that extracts heat from the water to warm the building

5 Operable windows and a large curtain wall allow extensive daylight to enter north-facing classrooms and the media center

6 Light shelves shade south-facing windows, which receive intense direct sunlight; operable windows below the light shelves provide natural ventilation

7 Vertical fins on the east- and west-facing glazing of the stair towers at the northeast and northwest corners of the school shade interior spaces from intense direct morning or afternoon sunlight, while permitting views and daylight into the spaces

8 Vertical fins on the east- and west-facing glazing of the stair towers at the northeast and northwest corners of the school shade interior spaces from intense direct morning or afternoon sunlight, while permitting views and daylight into the spaces

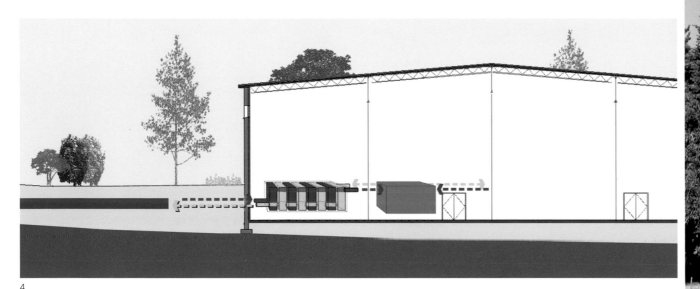

4

5

6

7

8

9

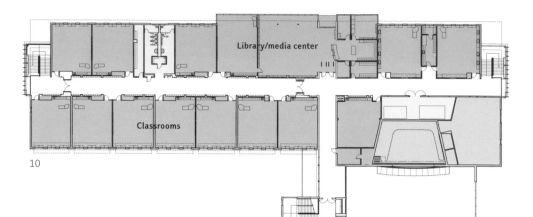

Library/media center

Classrooms

10

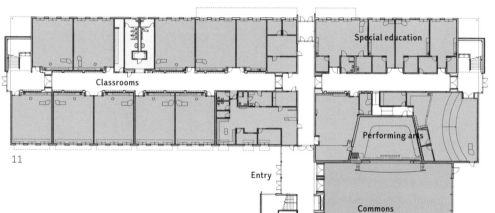

Classrooms

11

Special education

Performing arts

Entry

Commons

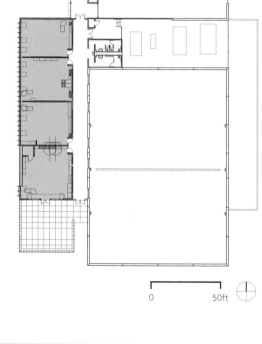

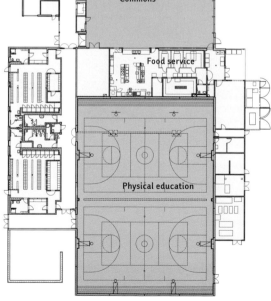

Food service

Physical education

9   A large curtain wall allows extensive
    daylight to enter the north-facing media
    center; operable windows provide daylight
    to north-facing classrooms

10 Second floor plan

11 First floor plan

12 The entry courtyard bridges the classroom
    wing that is oriented east-west for optimal
    solar control with the commons and arts
    and athletic spaces that are oriented
    north-south for optimal thermal control

0   50ft

12

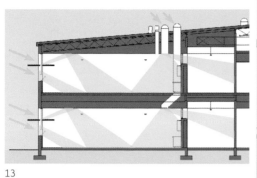

13

14

13 Building section at classroom wing showing daylighting path through windows, light shelves, Solatubes, and interior clerestories

14 Clerestories and interior glazing between the daylit media center and an adjacent hallway allow the hallway and the media center to share light

15 A typical, north-facing daylit classroom with light interior tones to help distribute daylight evenly; operable windows provide natural ventilation

Photography: Laurie Black for BOORA Architects

15

Trias VMBO School

Krommenie, The Netherlands
Atelier PRO architekten

■ Trias VMBO (pre-vocational secondary education) in Krommenie is a school for 1800 students. A separate sports center is located close to the school. The six building wings of the school are positioned perpendicular to the main volume; the spaces between the wings are protected by a glass roof, allowing them to serve as break or practice rooms.

The "Brink" is the binding element within the Trias VMBO, and is the entry for students and teachers before they disperse throughout the building. Ascending ramps on both ends create privacy; in addition, the stands and the galleries can be used during larger occasions, forming an amphitheater. The wings and the sectors show a prominent "face" toward the square.

The home base for the lower school students is designed with two floors around a light square where study stations and lockers are also located. The home base for the upper school students includes inspiring work and learning stations. These are shaped, as realistically as possible, as learning environments. Every sector has its own discussion and work space for the teaching staff and a room for private study.

By building a school and a sports center close together, a challenging connection is created. From the sports square there is a clear view into the different halls. The main sports hall, on the south side, is suitable for competitive sports and can also be split into three separate halls. A gymnasium, a hall for combat sports, a hall for gymnasts, and a fitness and aerobics room complete the sports center program.

The building combines high quality with a healthy indoor climate and minimum environmental effects. It functions like a three-dimensional exercise book, showing both students and teachers environmentally conscious techniques and thus adds to the value of daily education.

The building has been in use since mid-2006 and has already shown a 50 percent energy saving by comparison to the current new school buildings.

Sustainable features:

✿ Abundant daylight provided by glass surfaces in the rooms and aimed openings in the roof ✿ Low-temperature floor heating and high-temperature floor cooling via the concrete core form the basis of an energy-saving building with a very comfortable indoor environment ✿ A heat pump with ground storage forms the source for both heating and cooling ✿ For educational reasons, different forms of ventilation are used: in part of the building, natural ventilation is applied with an inflow of air via wind-pressure-dependent operating grids in the outer walls of the class rooms; in another section of the building a balance of ventilation with heat reclaiming is applied ✿ Winter gardens reduce energy consumption and require little maintenance ✿ 970 square feet (90 square meters) of solar panels on the roof of the sports center provide half the energy required for heating water for the showers ✿ Windmills are also installed to provide energy

1   Site plan

2   Model

3   Façade section

1

2

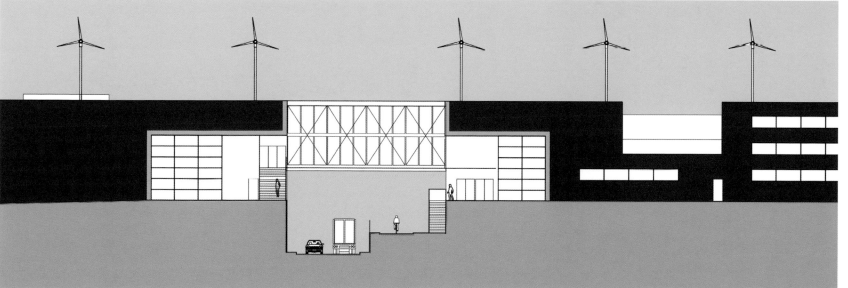

3

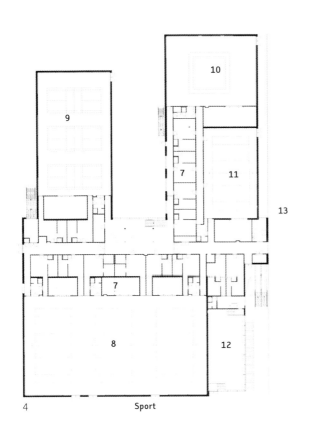

4   **Sport**

School

School

1   Main entrances
2   Foyer (atrium)
3   Classrooms
4   Winter garden
5   Technical classrooms
6   Amphitheater pavilion

Sport

7   Locker room
8   Sports hall
9   Gymnastics hall
10 Fight sports
11 Small sports hall
12 Fitness
13 Road

5

6

West Brazos Junior High School

Brazoria, Texas, USA
SHW Group LLP

■ West Brazos Junior High School is a 90,000-square-foot (8360-square-meter) facility that will house students in grades seven and eight. Its 53-acre (21.5-hectare) undeveloped, beautifully wooded site is approximately 57 miles (92 kilometers) south of Houston.

The building's dominant material is concrete masonry, chosen for its natural, durable quality. Stucco and metal panels complement the masonry to make a more economical structure without compromising durability and maintenance concerns. Natural colors of beiges, browns, and rusts, complemented by zero-maintenance clear anodized aluminum and energy-efficient green tinted glass allow the building to blend with the natural beauty of the heavily wooded campus.

A 260-foot (79-meter) circulation spine connects multiple learning/activity pod centers. These centers feature clerestory windows, allowing natural light deep into the core spaces. Landscaped courtyards provide generous views and natural light to the classrooms. Classroom windows feature low-E glazing and inexpensive shading devices that double as light shelves, distributing natural light further into learning spaces. Core spaces (library, dining area, and group instruction spaces) are also daylit, reducing artificial lighting loads, providing a visual link to the exterior spaces, reducing costly energy demands, lowering lifecycle costs, and ensuring that students and teachers can learn, work, and play in an open, fun, and liberating environment.

The site is preserved and consists of rainwater detention and natural filtration areas, and naturally preserved native landscape. All landscape elements added to the site, including spaces adjacent to the building, are filled with native grasses, bushes, and trees that are drought-resistant and thrive in the regional coastal environment.

Heat island effects are reduced through the use of a high-reflective Energy Star roofing system and reflective paving, which also reduce heat gains.

Once approved, West Brazos Junior High School will be the first public K–12 school in Texas to be LEED certified.

Sustainable features:

✿ Daylighting ✿ Shading ✿ Stormwater management ✿ Reflective roof surfacing ✿ Light-colored paving ✿ Native plants requiring no irrigation ✿ Exposed structure and systems ✿ Local materials ✿ 14.17% recycled materials ✿ Low-E glazing ✿ 31.31% water reduction ✿ Low emitting materials ✿ Light pollution reduction (no uplighting) ✿ Undisturbed wetlands ✿ Recycled 99.95% of construction waste ✿ Alternative transportation – bicycle storage/changing room and alternative fuel (electric) ✿ Carpool program (parking capacity)

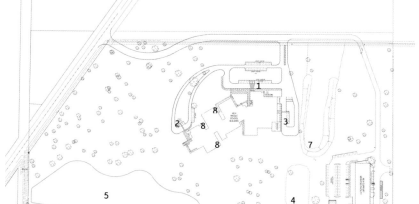

1   Site plan

2   Main entrance

1   Site plan

2   Main entrance

1   Parent drop-off/visitor parking
2   Special needs drop-off
3   Bus drop-off
4   Existing wetlands
5   Stormwater detention area
6   District support facility
7   Existing swale
8   Learning courtyard

1

2

1 Main entry
2 Administration
3 Library
4 Classrooms/activity rooms
5 Fine arts
6 Dining area
7 Gym
8 Science lab
9 Art classroom
10 Bus drop-off area
11 Learning courtyard

3

4

6

5

3   Floor plan

4   Every classroom has natural light; all
    classroom windows feature external shading
    devices to eliminate glare and heat gain

5   Major spaces are open and light-colored to
    encourage interaction between interior and
    exterior

6   Low-E insulated glass is used along with
    shading devices to allow daylight into all
    major spaces

7

8

7 The library is open-plan with study areas along exterior walls to take advantage of large windows

8 All classrooms feature daylighting

9 Exposed structure and systems stimulate curiosity in the library

10 Interior spaces have light-colored finishes to accent natural lighting

Photography: Richard Payne, FAIA

9

West Columbia Elementary School

West Columbia, Texas, USA
SHW Group LLP

Sustainable features:

⚙ Daylighting ⚙ Water collection ⚙ Native plantings ⚙ Reflective roofing materials ⚙ Light-colored paving ⚙ Window shading devices ⚙ Web-based systems controls ⚙ Structure and systems exposed as teaching tools ⚙ Local materials ⚙ Light pollution reduction ⚙ Low-E materials ⚙ Recycled construction materials ⚙ Alternative transportation facilities (bicycle storage and changing facilities)

■ This 95,600-square-foot (8882-square-meter) elementary school has a capacity for 800 students from Pre-K to grade six. Its 25-acre (10-hectare) site is approximately 55 miles (88.5 kilometers) south of Houston.

The sustainable strategies employed centered around water use, stormwater management, indoor environmental quality, and operational cost of the facility's mechanical and electrical systems. It was important to also take advantage of these strategies as on-site educational opportunities.

The natural landscape is preserved and landscape elements added to the site are drought-resistant native species that require no irrigation. Native plants in the landscape save water and maintenance while teaching students about their area's natural environment. The school has the capacity to capture rainwater from the roof and hold it in a cistern for educational use and to reduce stormwater runoff.

A critical factor for optimum learning is air quality. To avoid the use of traditional building materials that emit toxins, recycled building materials were used in the flooring material (VCT and carpet); paint, sealants, and adhesives with minimal off-gassing were also used. During the construction process building materials came from a radius of 50-100 miles (80-160 kilometers), cutting down on pollution caused by trucks shipping components across the country.

The orientation of the building, along with precise placement of shading devices, allows maximum light with minimal additional heat gain. This flood of natural light enhances learning and has no impact on operating costs. It also reduces the use of artificial lighting and reduces HVAC loads. The school district traded an upfront cost for web-based controls of HVAC systems, reducing energy use for unoccupied spaces. According to the school assistant superintendent, "... sustainable features give us an opportunity to invest in instruction, and that's really what we're all about. Sustainable design is a matter of good planning rather than spending money."

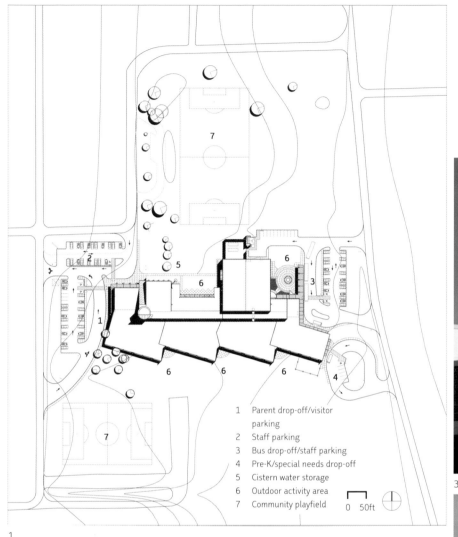

1 Parent drop-off/visitor
  parking
2 Staff parking
3 Bus drop-off/staff parking
4 Pre-K/special needs drop-off
5 Cistern water storage
6 Outdoor activity area
7 Community playfield

0   50ft

1 Site plan

2 Main entry

3 The solar clock is a main feature from outside the entry

4 Bike racks are adjacent to the main entry and
  administration for supervision

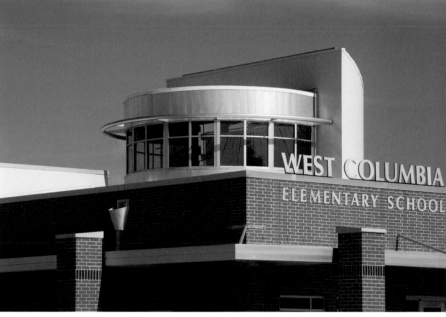

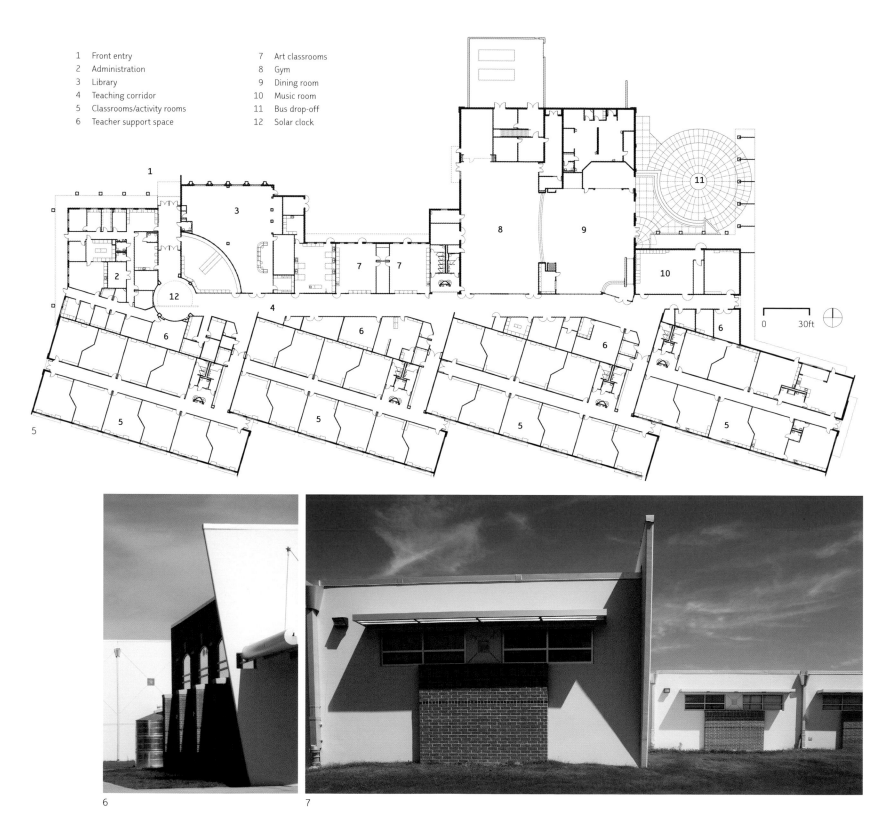

1 Front entry
2 Administration
3 Library
4 Teaching corridor
5 Classrooms/activity rooms
6 Teacher support space
7 Art classrooms
8 Gym
9 Dining room
10 Music room
11 Bus drop-off
12 Solar clock

0   30ft

5 Floor plan

6 Cisterns on the front of the buildings are used for irrigation

7 Classrooms feature high windows with exterior sun shades

8 Cisterns store rainwater collected from roofs for use in science experiments and artwork

8

10

9 Corridors become extensions of classrooms, with geometrical floor patterns, time-line graphics, maps, and display areas

10 Classrooms benefit from high windows that don't interrupt teaching walls

11 The library is daylit by large east-facing windows, allowing light deep into the space

12 Students learn about solar time using the solar clock

Photography: Richard Payne, FAIA

9

11

The Willow School

Gladstone, New Jersey, USA
Farewell Mills Gatsch Architects, LLC

■ The Willow School is a gold-level, LEED certified, K–8 independent school located on 34 acres (14 hectares) in Gladstone, New Jersey. This small private school was designed to reflect a curriculum rich in the lessons of environmental stewardship where children could experience a sense of wonder about the natural world and a connection to place. Built in phases, on a former 19th-century farm, each phase was designed to be perceived independently and yet be part of a complete whole. The program stresses the connection of indoor and outdoor spaces, use of the environment for learning opportunities, and the linkage of historical and contemporary experience.

Environmental stewardship has meant preserving both a historic farmstead as a piece of cultural history, conserving and stabilizing ecological zones such as wetlands and woodlands, and minimizing the impact of new construction on the natural ecosystems. The buildings are low and linear, with the long axis oriented east-west to respond to the sun and wind. The façade reveals a composition of local stone, salvaged heavy timbers, wood siding, and glass organized in agrarian structures along the spine of a sunspace corridor. The main entrance hall is used for morning gatherings of the entire school population. It fosters a strong sense of community and provides a location for community events after regular school hours. The light-filled classrooms, which spill off the corridor, have clear visual connections to the outside, making the link between learning and the world beyond the classroom walls readily apparent.

Sustainable features:

☼ Planting of native species meadows and reduction of areas of turf ☼ Marsh wetland stormwater management employing deep-rooted wetland plants to remove suspended solids, phosphorous, and nitrogen before stormwater leaves the site ☼ Constructed wetland treatment system treats human waste on site to recreational water standards ☼ Planting of species along waterways for erosion control ☼ Rainwater collection minimizes off-site stormwater ☼ Landscaped to encourage habitat diversity; planting of 40,000 diverse species to re-establish forest succession ☼ 30% water use reduction; toilets flushed with collected rainwater ☼ Optimization of energy efficiency to 40% better than ASHRAE 90.1-1999 code requirements ☼ Provision of south-facing sun space with concrete slab to store heat in winter and function as a heat sink in summer ☼ Operable windows with outdoor sensor that turns on lights when the temperature and humidity are conducive to opening the windows ☼ PV panels integrated on clerestory roofs; the 50 kW system produces approximately 14,000 kWh over the course of a year ☼ Electric light dimming system with photocell sensors ☼ Night purge ventilation to introduce cool air in spring and fall ☼ Waste management plan diverted 84% of construction debris from landfill ☼ Salvaged materials (heavy timbers and local stone) (20%) ☼ Recycled content (more than 20%) ☼ Preference given to locally harvested and manufactured products and materials (16%) ☼ Rapidly renewable linoleum and cork floor finish and Forbo tack boards (5%) ☼ Rediscovered structural wood framing from within 500 mile radius; all other wood reclaimed, rediscovered, or certified ☼ CO2 monitoring ☼ Low-VOC paints, adhesives, and sealants ☼ Non-toxic cleaning products

1   The master plan addressed site issues including woodlands, wetlands, setbacks, and circulation

2   The Willow School was carefully designed to harmonize with its woodland setting

3   Main entrance

1

2

3

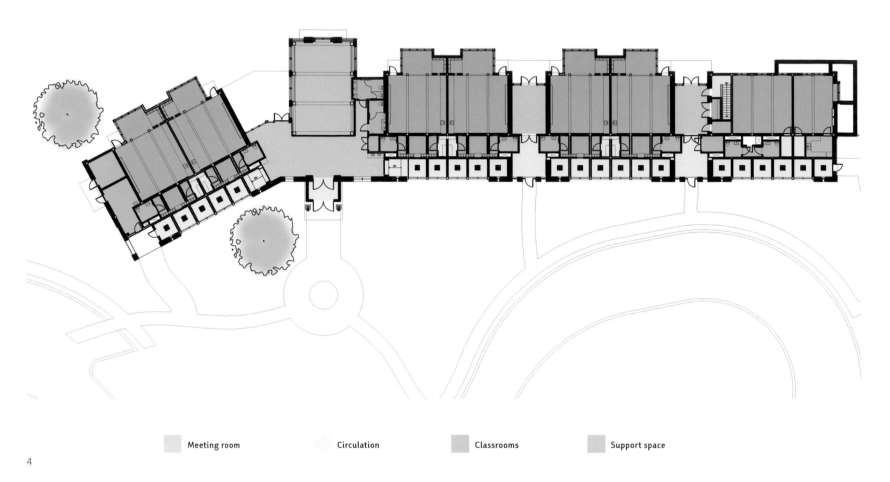

Meeting room	Circulation	Classrooms	Support space

4

5

4   Floor plan

5   The school building echoes the site's existing agrarian structures

6   Photovoltaic panels generate approximately 14,000 kWh over the course of one year

7   Study sketch for implementation of sustainable interventions

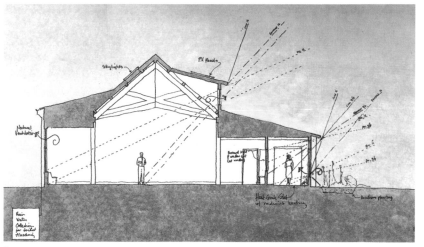

7

6

8

9

8 Corridors allow for plentiful daylight and fresh air

9 The main entrance hall, a gathering space for the entire school at the start of each day

10 Classrooms have direct access to the outdoors, reinforcing the curriculum's environmental emphasis

Photography: Taylor Photography (2,3,5,9); The Willow School (6,8,10)

10

WMEP Interdistrict Downtown School

Minneapolis, Minnesota, USA
Cuningham Group Architecture, P.A.

Sustainable features:

✿ Land, materials, and energy savings by locating the project downtown; by building vertically, land use was reduced by 95% ✿ More than 10% of the school program area is shared rather than built with corresponding savings in material use and energy consumption ✿ No gym floor equates to 100 maple trees still standing ✿ Open floor plan means fewer walls, greater flexibility, and a reduction in future remodeling needs ✿ Mechanical and electrical systems exposed, using less material and providing a learning opportunity; in addition, a ceiling did not need to be built ✿ Limited use of carpeting ✿ Linoleum in selected areas; all natural ingredients, biodegradable ✿ Air quality improved by operable windows, increased air exchanges, humidifying indoor air during heating cycles, locating fresh air intakes away from the loading dock, use of no- and low-VOC adhesives, paints and other interior finishes ✿ Desiccant heat recovery system decreases energy use; SolarWall™ panels used to preheat air ✿ Estimated overall energy savings are 40% compared to energy code ✿ All casework used Wheatboard™, a formaldehyde-free agricultural-based product ✿ Use of 75% recycled glass tile ✿ Rheinzinc and brick exterior with a 100-year life expectancy ✿ Demolition waste was recycled and construction waste reused where possible

■ This award-winning K–12 school is a multicultural learning center located in the heart of downtown Minneapolis and serves 11 Minnesota school districts that constitute the West Metro Education Program (WMEP). The project is a cooperative effort to establish an integrated, interdistrict magnet school for 600 students. The school's focus is to utilize the diverse downtown environment and its resources–to make appropriate use of advanced technologies, to support hands-on experiential learning, and to enhance multicultural learning, exchanges, and community building. The space program reflects this by providing focused instructional houses for student groups and shared whole-school space. The six instructional "houses" for the elementary, middle, and secondary levels are augmented with ancillary personnel and activity spaces.

The school takes advantage of its rich urban context by partnering with local business, government, and arts communities to provide students with off-site learning settings. Examples include sharing gym space with the YMCA, using the downtown library, and holding classes and performances at the nearby MacPhail Center for Music. The school is also connected to the University of St. Thomas School of Education and gives graduate students opportunities to teach and observe. Several businesses benefit as well through student internships and interaction. In addition to contributing to the sense of community, these partnerships allow the school to share space rather than build its own.

The school exemplifies many sustainable design techniques, including shared-use facilities and flexible space designed to minimize construction (the five-story school is built above a three-story below-grade municipal parking structure); energy design analysis to reduce consumption; and daylighting designed to reduce lighting and cooling loads. In addition, a transpired solar-wall heating system was integrated into the penthouse wall, sustainable materials were researched and selected, and sustainable construction waste management practices were specified.

1

2

1 View of urban context

2 School in relation to local
theater community

3 View of school showing
black SolarWall

3

4

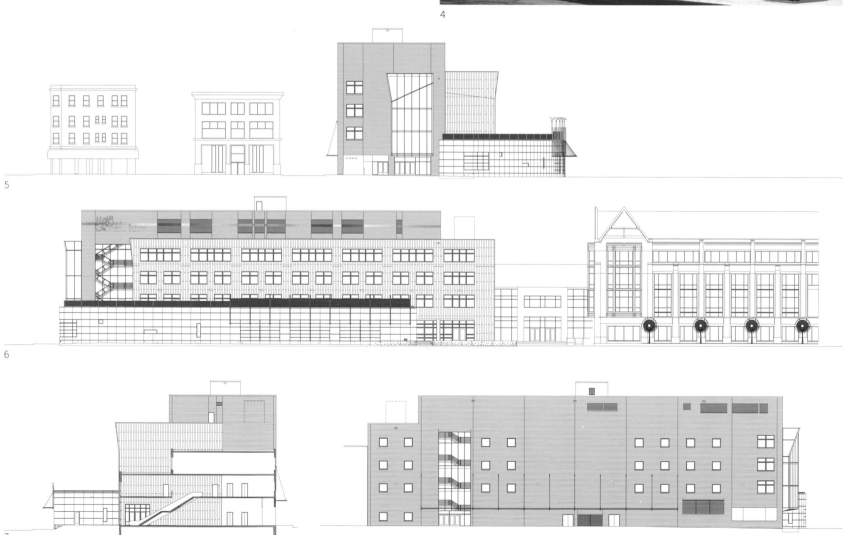

5

6

7

8

4 Connection to neighboring University School of Education

5-7 Elevations

8 Sunscreen along 10th Street façade

9 Interior stairwell

9

Home base
  1   Project area
  2   5-9 base unit
Shared space
  3   Multipurpose lab
  4   Arts lab
Administration
  5   Team area

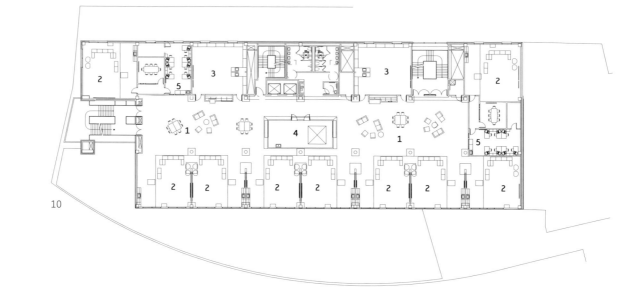

Shared space
  1   Library
  2   Big building lab
  3   Video
  4   Office
  5   Sound lab
  6   Storage
  7   K-5 kids lab
Gathering
  8   Display
Administration
  9   Welcome center
  10 Administration office
  11 Nurse
  12 Work room
Food service
  13 Food service

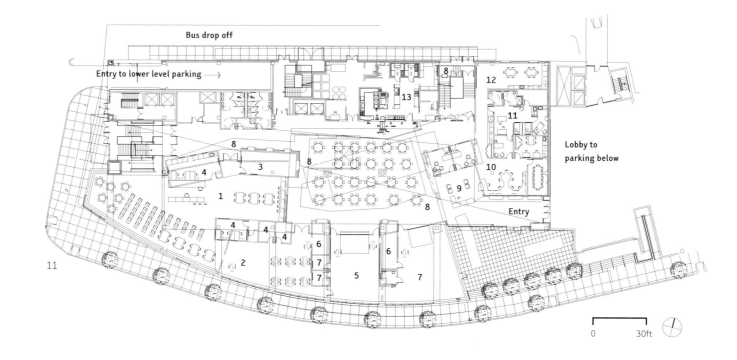

Bus drop off

Entry to lower level parking →

Lobby to parking below

Entry

0   30ft

12

10   Third floor plan

11   First floor plan

12   Whole school gathering space

13   Typical classroom space

Photography: Peter Kerze (1-4,8,9);
Don Wong (12,13)

13

Woodleigh School Science Building

Baxter, Victoria, Australia
Sean Godsell Architects

■ A 200- x 65-foot, (60- x 20-meter), single-story steel structure is embedded into the side of a gently sloping site to form the eastern edge of a new quadrangle at Woodleigh School. The simple portal frame, a combination of oxidized steel and ironbark, forms covered ways on the east and west sides of the building and doubles as a shading device. The building is designed as a "gallery of science" where the day-to-day activities of the users are on display for all to see; the aim is to stimulate and generate interest in the students by encouraging interaction. The classrooms become daily experiments in education, housed in a warm and nurturing environment and protected from the weather using sound design principles.

The building forms the eastern flank of the "north lawn," a new major outdoor space for senior students. The conventional quadrangle model of the original school is repeated in this gesture and the library becomes a pivotal building to both old and new outdoor spaces.

Five classrooms are accessed via a traditional covered way. A display and propagation greenhouse and an aquarium interrupt the rhythm of classroom modules. A staff resources room and HOD office terminate the prep room at the south end of the east side of the building, forming the staff entry to the building. A separate project room breaks away from the main building to form a covered outdoor teaching space.

The use of natural materials and introduction of natural light deep into the classrooms enhance the idea of a nurturing built environment, one that encourages learning and student interaction. The rigorous repetition of the timber and steel columns/shading device offers actual and symbolic protection of the internal environment. This was a deliberate biological analogy: the warm underbelly (endoskeleton) protected by the tough outer structure (exoskeleton).

Sustainable features:

✿ Rainwater harvesting ✿ Northern berm wall ✿ Recycled timber ✿ Fan-assisted natural ventilation of laboratory spaces ✿ Passive evaporative cooling ✿ All native (low water consuming and drought-tolerant) landscaping

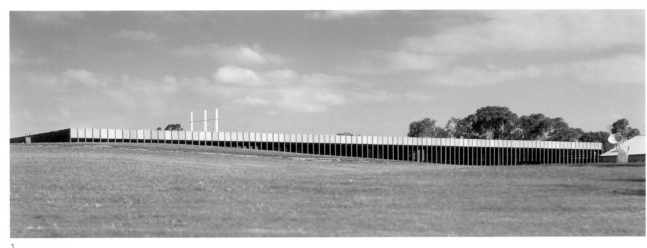

1 Exterior view

2 Exterior view through covered teaching space between the main building and project room

1

2

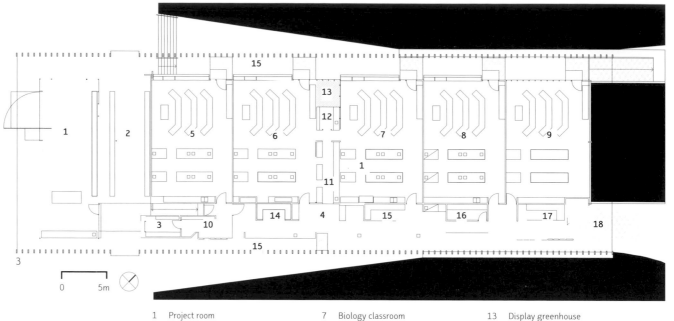

1	Project room	7	Biology classroom	13	Display greenhouse
2	Foyer	8	Chemistry classroom	14	General store
3	Office	9	Physics classroom	15	Biology store
4	Preparation room	10	Staff resource area	16	Hazchem store
5	General science classroom	11	Aquarium	17	Physics store
6	Junior/marine biology	12	Greenhouse	18	Loading bay

4

3 Floor plan

4 Exterior view

5 Classroom interior

5

6   Entry portal

7   Project room interior

8   Repeated timber and steel columns form a covered way on the
    east and west sides of the building

Photography: Hayley Franklin

6

7

8

Woodward Academy Middle School

College Park, Georgia, USA
Perkins+Will

■ The new campus for the Woodward Academy Middle School includes a new classroom building, dining hall, and arts building, all enclosing a middle school quadrangle.

In an effort to relate to the small-scale houses adjacent and across the street from the new classroom building, the building scale was decreased by expressing the classrooms as small pavilions. The glass third floor of the building steps back from the brick façade, giving the facility a two-story reading in keeping with the neighboring homes.

The dining hall faces east and opens onto the quad with a tree-covered patio that will accommodate outdoor dining. The arts building is to the northwest of the dining hall. All the art classrooms face north and have full glass walls to allow natural light into the rooms.

The facility has been LEED certified for its sustainable design. It is the first K-12 LEED certified project in Georgia. The facility is heated and cooled by a geothermal field of piping extending under the courtyard in front of the building; the building is oriented north-south for maximum energy efficiency, and many recyclable finish materials were used. Stormwater management strategies incorporated in the project include bioretention gardens in the landscape design that clean the water and serve as detention facilities as well as the use of a green roof on the art building.

Sustainable features:

⚙ Geothermal heating and cooling ⚙ North-south orientation for energy efficiency ⚙ Use of recycled finish materials ⚙ Stormwater management strategies

1　Courtyard with greenspace

2　Tree shading

3　Exterior with greenspace

4

6

5

7

8   Art studio with daylighting

9   Interior daylighting

Photography: Chris Little Photography (1-4,9); courtesy Perkins+Will (5-8)

8

9

Appendix

Resources

The following websites contain more information and links to further resources on sustainability. Some of the websites are geared specifically to schools; others provide more general or related information. Links are also available via www.huttonford.com. Thanks to Kerrie Kannberg, LEED AP, who assisted in the compilation of this list.

General sites

www.aia.org/cae_default
The American Institute of Architects' Committee on Architecture for Education (CAE) consists of AIA members and allied professionals concerned with the quality of educational facility design.

www.anfarch.org
Academy of Neuroscience for Architecture (ANFA). The mission of the Academy is to promote and advance knowledge that links neuroscience research to a growing understanding of human responses to the built environment.

www.ases.org
Website of the American Solar Energy Society, a national organization whose mission is to attain a sustainable U.S. energy economy. A resource for information on solar and other renewable energies.

www.cap-e.com/ewebeditpro/items/O59F9819.pdf
Report: *Greening America's Schools – Costs and Benefits* by Gregory Kats.

www.cefpi.org
The Council of Educational Facility Planners (CEFPI), an advocate for excellence in student learning environments.

www.chps.net
The website of the Collaborative for High Performance Schools (CHPS), whose mission is to improve the quality of education and facilitate the design of high-performance learning environments.

www.corrim.org
Journal of the Society of Wood Science and Technology, a consortium for research on renewable industrial materials.

www.earthteam.net
An environmental network for teens, teachers, and youth leaders; a good resource for teachers.

www.ecosmartinc.com
Online catalog of high-performance design products.

www.edcmag.com
Website of *Environmental Design + Construction* magazine, which touches all building types, including education.

www.educationdesignshowcase.com
Case studies of primary, secondary, and higher education projects.

www.envirolink.org
An online environmental resource with links to a variety of websites and articles.

www.globalgreen.org/greenbuilding
General green building website for cities and schools.

www.greenerbuilding.org

Source for sustainable building products and ideas.

www.greenfloors.com

Reference information on a variety of environmentally friendly flooring products.

www.life-cycle.org

Life cycle analysis links.

www.nrel.gov/docs/fy00osti/28049.pdf

Study by the National Renewable Energy Laboratory (NREL): *Daylighting in Schools: Improving Student Performance and Health at a Price Schools can Afford.*

www.oikos.com/green_products/index.php

Contact information for a variety of manufacturers of green building products.

www.pefc.org/internet/html

Website of the PEFC (Programme for the Endorsement of Forest Certification schemes), a global umbrella organization for the assessment and mutual recognition of national forest certification schemes.

www.pge.com/003_save_energy/003c_edu_train/pec/daylight/di_pubs/SchoolDetailed820App.PDF

Study on daylighting in schools undertaken on behalf of the California Board for Energy Efficiency.

www.pprc.org/pubs/schools/biblio.cfm

Bibliography of publications related to sustainable design for schools.

www.rebuild.gov

Rebuild America is a program committed to saving energy, improving building performance, easing air pollution and enhancing the quality of life through energy efficiency and renewable energy technologies. A program of The U.S. Department of Energy.

www.recycle-steel.org

The Steel Recycling Institute (SRI) promotes and sustains the recycling of all steel products. Also serves as an education resource.

www.rmi.org

The Rocky Mountain Institute (RMI) is an independent, entrepreneurial nonprofit organization. It fosters the efficient and restorative use of resources.

www.sustainableschools.dgs.ca.gov/SustainableSchools

Part of the California state architect website, which includes information on a variety of sustainable design issues and links to other related websites.

www.USGBC.org

Website of the U.S. Green Building Council, whose mission is to make sustainability the foundation of the building marketplace. Includes information on LEED (Leadership in Energy and Environmental Design) system.

www.worldchanging.com

A comprehensive website based on the book, Worldchanging: *A User's Guide for the 21st Century.* Contains links to archival material specifically related to schools.

International sites

www.aries.mq.edu.au/pdf/international_review.pdf

An international review of whole-school sustainability programs.

www.c2p2online.com

Canadian Center for Pollution Prevention.

www.cagbc.com

Website of the Canada Green Building Council, a coalition of representatives from different segments of the design and building industry.

www.ciionline.org

India's Sustainable Council.

www.designshare.com

Extensive website covering a large range of issues related to school facility design. Includes an extensive database of projects from around the world with photographs, project descriptions, narratives, and project teams.

www.edfacilities.org/rl/school_design_international.cfm

National Clearinghouse for Educational Facilities (NCEF). NCEF provides a resource list of links, books, and articles on educational facilities outside the US and UK.

www.efseurope.org

European-based website promoting education and sustainability.

www.fee-international.org/

The Foundation for Environmental Education (FEE) is a non-government, non-profit organization with member organizations in 47 countries promoting sustainable development through environmental education.

www.iclei.org

ICLEI - Local Governments for Sustainability is an international association of local governments and national and regional local government organizations that have made a commitment to sustainable development.

www.iisbe.org

International Initiative for a Sustainable Built Environment (iiSBE) focuses on energy and environmental issues in the building sector.

www.inforse.dk

Website of INFORSE, the International Network for Sustainable Energy. Features educational links, predominantly energy-based.

www.ises.org

The International Solar Energy Society (ISES) was established in 1954 to serve the needs of the renewable energy community. An information resource on renewable energy.

www.unep.or.jp/ietc/sbc/Resource_Link.asp

United Nations Environment Programme: sustainable building and construction forum.

www.worldgbc.org

The World Green Building Council aims to be the peak global not-for-profit organization working to transform the property industry toward sustainability through its members: national Green Building Councils.

About the author

Alan Ford, AIA

Alan Ford, AIA, is a principal with Hutton Ford Architects P.C. He has designed more than 75 K–12 high-performance school projects and is co-author of the book *A Sense of Entry*, published by The Images Publishing Group in 2007.

A licensed architect with 28 years of experience, Alan has a Bachelor of Environmental Design and a Master of Architecture from the University of Colorado. Prior to forming Hutton Ford Architects with Paul Hutton in 1993, he worked with architectural firms W.C. Muchow & Partners, Kohn Pedersen Fox Architects, and John Burgee Architects with Philip Johnson. Alan served on the editorial board of the award-winning AIA magazine *Architect Colorado* from 2005 to 2007 and has been a frequent honorarium professor and guest critic at the University of Colorado, School of Architecture since 1977.

Acknowledgments

The concept for this book originated with Paul Latham and Alessina Brooks of The Images Publishing Group—thank you for your vision and support in advancing our knowledge on this very important topic. Coordinating editor Robyn Beaver's insights and assistance in managing the content for the book have been invaluable.

I would also like to thank all of the architects and photographers for their generosity in providing materials for the book. Their willingness to share their first-hand experience in designing the sustainable school will benefit all of us interested in creating better schools.

A number of individuals and organizations were willing to share their knowledge and project recommendations to be considered for the book. Thanks to Paul Hutton of Hutton Ford Architects, Randall Fielding of Design Share, Lance Hosey and Mark Rylander of William McDonough + Partners, Betsy del Monte of The Beck Group, and The American Institute of Architects.

Finally, a special thanks to John P. Eberhard, FAIA, and Rick Fedrizzi, CEO of USGBC, for their willingness to share their expertise in writing pieces for this book. Their leadership in advancing and promoting the issues presented here is extraordinary.